W9-CFB-395

mozart

compact companions

PHILIPS *Classics*

COMPACT COMPANIONS

MOZART

NEIL WENBORN

SIMON & SCHUSTER

NEW YORK LONDON TORONTO SYDNEY TOKYO SINGAPORE

SIMON & SCHUSTER
ROCKEFELLER CENTER
1230 AVENUE OF THE AMERICAS
NEW YORK, NEW YORK 10020

Designed by Wherefore Art? Edited by Emma Lawson

Printed in Singapore by Imago Publishing Ltd
10 9 8 7 6 5 4 3 2 1

Library of Congress Cataloging-in-Publication Data
Wenborn, Neil.
Mozart : a listener's guide to the classics / by Neil Wenborn.
p. cm. — (Compact companions)
Discography: p.
ISBN 0-671-88791-2
1. Mozart, Wolfgang Amadeus, 1756–1791. 2. Composers—Austria—Biography. I. Title. II. Series.
ML410.M9W42 1994
780'.92—dc20
[B] 93-39718
CIP
MN

CONTENTS

Mozart's birthplace in the Getreidegasse, Salzburg:
the Mozarts' flat was on the third floor

The Child Prodigy

'I must inform you,' Leopold Mozart wrote to his Augsburg publisher in February 1756, 'that on January 27, at 8 pm, my dear wife was happily delivered of a boy.' The child, the seventh to be born to Leopold and Maria Anna Mozart of Salzburg but only the second to survive, was to change not only his parents' lives but also the course of musical history. Before long Leopold himself would call him 'the miracle God caused to be born in Salzburg'.

At the time, though, Leopold's thoughts were equally occupied with another delivery. He was in the final stages of seeing through the press his *magnum opus* on violin technique, the *Versuch einer gründlichen Violinschule* (Essay on the fundamentals of violin-playing). The work was published in the summer to warm reviews and carried Leopold's name far beyond the confines of provincial Salzburg. It was widely translated and reprinted both during and after the eighteenth century – it is still an invaluable source for 'authentic' interpreters today – and would have assured its author a place in musical history even if he had not been the father of his son.

Leopold Mozart, born in Augsburg in 1719, was the son of a bookbinder. While his brother remained in the family business, he went to Salzburg as a law and philosophy student in 1737. Two years later, at the age of twenty, he dropped out of his studies and took up the post of musician and valet (a common combination in the musical world into which Mozart was born) to a leading ecclesiastic, the Count of Thurn and Taxis. He advanced steadily through the Salzburg musical hierarchy, becoming a violin teacher at the cathedral choir school and eventually, seven years after his son's birth, deputy Kapellmeister (deputy director of music) at the court of the Prince-Archbishop.

His prolific output as a composer includes both secular and sacred works, a reflection of the fact that the archbishopric was both a temporal and an ecclesiastical jurisdiction. In 1747 Leopold married Maria Anna Pertl, the daughter of a senior local official; in their prime the couple were spoken of as the most handsome in Salzburg. Their daughter Maria Anna, known universally by the affectionate diminutive 'Nannerl', was born in 1751 and showed remarkable musical talent from an early age. Within a few years, however, her abilities would be overshadowed by those of her younger brother.

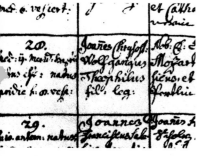

Salzburg baptismal register, giving Mozart's name as Joannes Chrysost{omus} Wolfgangus Theophilus

'THE MIRACLE GOD CAUSED TO BE BORN IN SALZBURG'

The day after his birth in the Mozarts' third-floor apartment in the Getreidegasse, the new baby was christened Joannes Chrysostomus Wolfgangus Theophilus. Like so many documents from his later life, the baptismal certificate already explodes a myth: 'Amadeus' features nowhere on it. The Latin form of Theophilus ('beloved of God'), it was hardly ever used by Mozart himself, who preferred 'Amadè' or 'Amadé' when he was feeling Mediterraneanly inclined and 'Gottlieb' when he wasn't. In the family he was known as Wolfgang or, in the early years, by variants of 'Woferl'.

Most of the stories about Wolfgang's earliest childhood date from much later, but it is clear that his precocious musical gifts were apparent from an astonishingly young age. Three days before his son's fifth birthday, for example, Leopold noted below a scherzo in Nannerl's musical exercise book: 'This piece was learnt by Wolfgangerl on January 24, 1761 . . . between 9 and 9:30 in the evening', and similar notes followed over the next few days. Nannerl later recalled how her brother would sit at the keyboard picking out thirds and playing them, and the Salzburg court trumpeter, Johann Andreas Schachtner, a close family friend, remembered in touchingly plausible detail how he and Leopold had returned from church one day to find the little boy scribbling away at what he claimed to be a clavier concerto:

Leopold Mozart in 1765

His father took it from him and showed me a smudge of notes, most of which were written over ink-blots which he had rubbed out. . . . At first we laughed at what seemed such a galimatias, but his father then began to observe the most important matter, the notes and music; he stared long at the sheet, and then tears, tears of joy and wonder, fell from his eyes. Look, Herr Schachtner, {he} said, see how correctly and properly it is all written, only it can't be used, for it is so very difficult that no one could play it. Wolfgangerl said: That's why it's a concerto, you must practice it till you can get it right, look, that's how it goes. He played, and managed to get just enough out of it for us to see what he intended.

Schachtner also recalled Wolfgang's fascination with arithmetic, his ability to detect minute discrepancies in the tuning of two violins and his terror of the sound of a trumpet. Nannerl confirmed that her brother was already composing little pieces at the age of five and playing them to their father to write down.

Leopold was not only a man with a keen sense of responsibility for the development of what he saw as his son's God-given gifts; he was also a businessman of initiative and imagination. From the moment Wolfgang's extraordinary abilities revealed themselves, he abandoned some of his own musical activities to concentrate on promoting those of his children to a wider public. Accordingly, in January 1762, he obtained a three-week leave of absence from his employer, Archbishop Schrattenbach, to visit Munich, where Wolfgang and Nannerl played the harpsichord before the Elector of Bavaria.

It was the first of the many musical journeys which would take up much of Mozart's childhood. By the late summer of 1762 Leopold was planning another trip, this time to the very hub of the Habsburg empire.

The Mozarts on tour

On September 18, 1762 Leopold, Maria Anna, Nannerl and the six-year-old Wolfgang set off from Salzburg for Vienna, where Leopold planned to parade the children's talents before the nobility and, with luck, the royal family itself. After spending a few days at Passau, where Wolfgang played at the home of a local dignitary, the itinerant family concert party sailed down the Danube to Linz, where they stayed at an inn run by two spinsters named Kiener. It was here, on October 1, that Wolfgang gave his first solo public performance. Five days later, already preceded by their reputation, the family arrived in Vienna and began a glittering round of visits to the nobility, during which the children showed off their musical skills to general astonishment. Writing home to their Salzburg landlord, Hagenauer, Leopold reported that 'everyone is amazed, especially at the boy, and everyone whom I have heard says that his genius is incomprehensible'.

Wolfgang and Nannerl playing before the Empress Maria Theresa, a romanticized nineteenth-century view

The highlights of the trip, however, were two audiences with the Empress Maria Theresa and other members of her family (including the seven-year-old Marie Antoinette, who would marry Louis XVI of France and be guillotined during the French Revolution). After performing on the first occasion, Wolfgang, with the affectionate openness that was to be commented on by almost all who encountered him on these childhood tours, leapt onto the Empress's lap, threw his arms around her neck and kissed her. Apparently unoffended, she later sent him a lilac and gold braid gala-costume (actually a cast-off from her son, the Archduke Maximilian), which he wore for a charming formal portrait by Pietro Lorenzoni.

Apart from the fact that Wolfgang suffered from intermittent bouts of illness on this trip, no doubt exacerbated by what Leopold called 'our irregular life, early rising, eating and drinking at all hours, and wind and rain', the tour was an enormous success, and the family returned to Salzburg in January 1763 both better known and better off than when they had left almost three months before. A few weeks later, Leopold was promoted to deputy Kapellmeister at Salzburg – the highest rank he was ever to attain – and was soon planning another, more ambitious, journey. Once again, Archbishop Schrattenbach magnanimously granted his new deputy Kapellmeister extended leave of absence and on June 9, 1763 the whole family, together with a servant, Sebastian Winter, set out in their own carriage on the longest of all Mozart's childhood tours.

THE GREAT EUROPEAN JOURNEY

This third journey, which was to take them to Germany, France, England, the Netherlands and Switzerland, would keep them away from home for the next three-and-a-half years. Their itinerary, which was designed to take in most of Europe's important musical centers, makes exhausting reading even today. Given the rigors of eighteenth-century travel, with its barely sprung carriages, dangerous and often impassable roads and relatively primitive accommodation, it was a remarkable feat both of endurance and of organization. Leopold, Nannerl and Wolfgang were all dangerously ill at different times during these tours, and it is testimony to their strength and determination (and a case against the romanticized picture of Mozart as a delicate hothouse flower) that they survived at all. That they were able to perform to general acclaim at every stage of their travels, often within hours of their arrival, is little short of amazing.

Their first main port of call on the present journey was Munich, where the children played at court. They then continued, giving concerts and private performances at the homes of the nobility as they went, to Frankfurt, where on August 12 Leopold left a graffito scratched on the windowpane of their lodging house in the Bendergasse (the inscription 'Mozart Maitre de la Musique

A liberal employer: Siegmund Christoph von Schrattenbach, Prince-Archbishop of Salzburg

de la Chapelle de Salzbourg avec Sa Famile [sic] le 12 Aout 1763' can still be seen in the Frankfurt Historical Museum.) Six days later, the children gave a public concert, an experience which at least one member of the audience – the fourteen-year-old Goethe – could still vividly recall more than sixty years later, describing 'the little fellow with his wig and his sword' to a friend in 1830. By the first week of October they were in Brussels and by mid-November in Paris, where they were to stay for five months. Here they were granted the rare privilege of giving public concerts and performing privately before Louis XV at Versailles; they were also permitted to attend the royal table at dinner, though they were obliged to stand throughout, the Queen passing food to Wolfgang from her plate as she talked to him. When Mozart's first published works, four sonatas for harpsichord and violin (a combination popular with amateur music makers), appeared in the spring as Opus I and Opus II, they were dedicated, in conventionally elaborate fashion, to one of the king's daughters and a lady-in-waiting. In the numbering system created by the nineteenth-century mineralogist Köchel, by whose initial Mozart's works are now designated, they appear as K6–9.

'PRODIGIES OF NATURE'

The main features of the children's act can be reconstructed from the many surviving accounts of their performances. Nannerl was often praised as the more accomplished clavier player, but everywhere her skills were eclipsed by the precocious, all-around musicianship of her younger brother. Wolfgang would demonstrate his sight-reading abilities, add a bass to a melody at sight and vice versa, name notes played to him from an adjacent room, play the clavier faultlessly even when the keyboard was covered by a cloth, transpose pieces into another key at sight, and improvise on themes given to him by members of the audience, often at length and, as his musical knowledge increased, in strict and difficult forms such as the fugue.

Even in an age of prodigies – and the Mozarts' path crossed those of various other *Wunderkinder* in their travels – it is clear that the young Wolfgang made an exceptional impression on his audiences. Baron Friedrich Melchior von Grimm, who was to become an invaluable family friend (until Mozart had a falling out with him in later life), heard him in Paris in December 1763, and his account of his first exposure to this unnerving talent is worth quoting at some length for the sense of awe it still conveys after more than 200 years:

'Prodigies of nature': Leopold, Wolfgang and Nannerl in their Paris publicity portrait, 1763

True prodigies are sufficiently rare to be worth speaking of, when you have had occasion to see one. A Kapellmeister of Salzburg, Mozart by name, has just arrived here with two children who cut the prettiest figure in the world. His daughter, eleven years of age, plays the

*Mozart's sister, Maria Anna ('Nannerl'),
painted in 1763*

*harpsichord in the most brilliant manner. . . . Her brother,
who will be seven years old next February, is such an
extraordinary phenomenon that one is hard put to it to believe
what one sees with one's eyes and hears with one's ears. It
means little for this child to perform with the greatest precision
the most difficult pieces, with hands that can hardly stretch a
sixth; but what is really incredible is to see him improvise for
an hour on end and in doing so give rein to the inspiration of
his genius and to a mass of enchanting ideas, which moreover
he knows how to connect with taste and without confusion.
The most consummate Kapellmeister could not be more
profound than he in the science of harmony and of
modulations, which he knows how to conduct by the least
expected but always accurate paths . . . but here is something
more I have seen, which is no less incomprehensible. A woman
asked him the other day whether he was able to accompany by ear, and without looking at it,
an Italian cavatina she knew by heart; and she began to sing. The child tried a bass that was
not absolutely correct, because it is impossible to prepare in advance the accompaniment to a song
one does not know; but when the tune was finished, he asked her to begin again, and at this
repeat he not only played the whole melody of the song with the right hand, but with the other
added the bass without hesitation; whereafter he asked {her} ten times to begin again, and at
each repeat he changed the style of his accompaniment; and he could have repeated this twenty
times, if he had not been stopped. I cannot be sure that this child will not turn my head if I go
on hearing him often; he makes me realize that it is difficult to guard against madness on
seeing prodigies.*

No less touching is Leopold's own growing sense of wonder at his son's accomplishments, a wonder often couched in deeply religious tones. (For all his anti-authoritarian sniping and his deep interest in Mammon, Leopold remained a devout, not to say superstitious, Catholic.) The boy's mastery of the organ on this trip becomes 'a fresh act of God's grace which many a one only receives after much labor; and 'every day', (he wrote from Paris) 'God performs fresh miracles through this child'. Leopold was already building up an archive of materials for a projected biography of his son (which in the event was never written), and it seems likely that the voluminous and immensely colorful letters he wrote home to their Salzburg landlord Hagenauer, detailing the giant strides Wolfgang was making from day to day and the rapture with which he was everywhere received, were intended to be preserved.

There is something profoundly moving about Leopold's awe-struck tributes to Wolfgang's extraordinary gifts. Whatever the later difficulties in their relationship, this admiration was never to diminish,

The Wunderkind: Mozart, aged seven, wearing the suit given him by the Empress Maria Theresa

and to the end, amid the increasing disaffection of Leopold's life, the unrivaled perfection of his son's music could still move him to tears.

LONDON

In April 1764, the whole family (minus Sebastian Winter, who had found more exalted employment at a princely court) left Paris for Calais, and towards the end of the month they crossed the Channel to England. It was the first time any of them had seen the sea, and Leopold reports Wolfgang's fascination with the way the water moved backwards and forwards, as well as the fact that they were all horribly seasick. On the twenty-third they arrived in London, which they were to make their home for more than a year.

The nine-year-old Mozart's manuscript of the chorus 'God is my refuge', corrected by Leopold

Once again Leopold exhibited his natural flair for publicity. Within five days of their arrival they had been presented at court, where the children performed before George III (then a young man of twenty-seven) and his consort Queen Charlotte. The royal family received them with even greater friendliness than t[...]e continent (though Leopold cannot forbear to mention that th[...]y twenty-four guineas for their pains!) A week later, as Leopold report[...]er, the Mozarts were walking in St. James's Park when 'the King came d[...]g with the Queen and, although we all had on different clothes, they recogn[...]evertheless and not only greeted us, but the King opened the window, leaned[...]and saluted us and especially our Master Wolfgang, nodding to us and waving his hand.'

London: the interior of the
Rotunda in Ranelagh Gardens

There were public concerts too, which were well attended and consequently highly profitable, even though the London 'season' was officially over. (Leopold, with his keen eye for business, knew that the King's birthday on June 4 would bring the nobility back to town and had had advertisements placed in the press, promoting his 'prodigies of nature' on the back of their reception at court.) As usual, Wolfgang's performances were a triumph. Leopold told Hagenauer that the progress the boy had made since leaving Salzburg beggared imagination, and that he was now planning an opera he wanted to produce with his friends in Salzburg. The theatrical ambitions that were to bear fruit in the great operas of Mozart's last decade were already stirring.

On June 29, at Ranelagh House, a renowned pleasure garden by the River Thames, Wolfgang performed some of his own compositions for the harpsichord and organ at a fund-raising concert in aid of a new maternity hospital, Leopold slyly calculating that charitable acts are 'one way of winning the affection of this quite exceptional nation'. The advertisement, this time apparently not drafted by Leopold himself, hyped the eight-year-old as 'the most extraordinary Prodigy, and the most amazing Genius that has appeared in any Age' and, as with most such notices at this time, understated his age by a year.

In August this run of success was interrupted when Leopold became seriously ill and the family moved from their lodgings in St. Martin's Lane to the more salubrious surroundings of Chelsea, then a riverside village a few miles from London. There, at what is now 180 Ebury Street, Wolfgang, unable to play the harpsichord for fear of disturbing the invalid, amused himself writing his first symphonies (K16 and K19), Nannerl recording in later years how he asked her to remind him to give the horn plenty to do.

By the end of September they were back in town and resuming their public musical life. There was another appearance at court (their third and last), the publication of another set of sonatas (this time dedicated to the Queen), and meetings with leading figures of London musical life, including J. C. Bach (son of the great Johann Sebastian) who was to be an enduring influence on the young Mozart. And there were more concerts and private performances, at which Wolfgang continued to allay the scepticism that often preceded him, passing with flying colors the tests Leopold encouraged musicians to put to him at their lodgings.

One such examiner was the philosopher Daines Barrington, who met the Mozarts in June 1765 and later submitted his report on Wolfgang to the Royal Society. Like Grimm's, his account has a startling immediacy, as when, having asked the child to improvise 'a *Song of Rage*, such as might be proper for the opera stage', he describes how Wolfgang 'looked back with much archness, and began five or six lines of a jargon recitative proper to precede a *Song of Anger*' before launching himself into an aria in the middle of which he 'worked himself up to such a pitch, that he beat his harpsichord like a person possessed, rising sometimes in his chair'. Again, describing how Mozart played and sung a duet with Leopold at sight, he tells us that 'his father, who took the under part in this duet, was once or twice out, though the passages were not more difficult than those in the upper one; on which occasions the son looked back with some anger pointing out to him his mistakes, and setting him right'.

Touchingly, Barrington also quotes as evidence for Wolfgang's not being older than Leopold claimed the fact that 'he had not only a most childish appearance, but likewise had all the actions of that stage of life. For example, whilst he was playing to me, a favourite cat came in, upon which he immediately left his harpsichord, nor could we bring him back for a considerable time.' Before the family finally left London at the end of July 1765 the children embarked on a grueling schedule of daily performances at the Swan and Harp tavern in Cornhill as Leopold sought to squeeze the last financial benefits out of an already extremely profitable stay. A natural adept at what modern marketing agencies would call merchandising, he was even offering for sale engraved copies of the group publicity portrait he had had done in Paris.

HOMEWARD BOUND

After a week staying in a country house near Canterbury the Mozarts braved the Channel again at the beginning of August and made their way to the Netherlands. Both Wolfgang and Leopold had been ill *en route*, but at the Hague Nannerl went down with a far more serious condition. For almost two months she lay dangerously ill with intestinal typhoid and in October was given extreme unction. In a letter to Hagenauer of November 5, 1765 Leopold paints a moving picture of the family as they sat anxiously at her bedside, though there is also more than a hint of the almost chilling detachment with which Mozart, throughout his life, was able to immerse himself in his own musical world:

> *Whoever could have listened to the conversations which we three, my wife, myself and my daughter, had on several evenings, during which we convinced [Nannerl] of the vanity of this world and the happy death of children, would not have heard it without tears. Meanwhile little Wolfgang in the next room was amusing himself with his music.*

No sooner was Nannerl out of danger than Wolfgang himself collapsed with the same disease, though he had recovered sufficiently by the end of the year to have resumed composition and was able to perform again in public almost immediately upon the family's arrival in Amsterdam in January.

1766 saw the Mozart party making its way slowly back to Salzburg via the Austrian Netherlands (Belgium), France, Switzerland and Germany, with the usual round of public appearances and performances at noble houses and royal courts. In Paris Baron

Grimm again heard the children play and was amazed at the progress they had made since their visit on the outgoing leg of their grand tour two years earlier. 'If these children live,' he wrote, 'they will not remain at Salzburg. Before long monarchs will vie for their possession.' Tragically, Mozart's adult career was to prove the latter prediction all too hollow.

SALZBURG AND VIENNA

Wolfgang, Leopold, Nannerl and Maria Anna arrived back in Salzburg on November 29, 1766. During their three-and-a-half years away from home they had amassed a great deal more than plaudits. The librarian of St. Peter's Abbey, Beda Hübner, visited the Mozarts' apartment a few days after their return and recorded in his diary that it was like inspecting a church treasury, so numerous were the gold watches, snuffboxes, jewelery etc. they had been presented with on their travels. Hübner estimated the value of these gifts alone as some 12,000 florins (Leopold's annual Salzburg salary was 350 florins).

Most important of all for Mozart's development, though, was the wide range of contemporary musical influences to which he had been exposed during his most impressionable years in the course of their travels. In the nine months Wolfgang now spent at home before the family set off on their next tour, the Salzburg court was to see and hear the fruits of that experience at first hand.

At the beginning of 1767, the Archbishop invited Wolfgang to write the first act of

Salzburg's Lent production, *Die Schuldigkeit des ersten Gebots*, a musical meditation on the text of the first commandment. Since secular theatrical works of any kind were expressly forbidden during Lent, it had become standard practice for composers to apply operatic conventions to sacred texts at this season of the year, and the commission therefore gave Mozart the opportunity he had been dreaming of since London to try his hand at operatic writing. With its elaborate arias, designed to show off the performers' vocal skills to best advantage, *Die Schuldigkeit* K35 demonstrates the eleven-year-old's facility for imitating the conventions of *opera seria* (literally 'serious opera', as against *opera buffa* – 'comic opera') and is his first large-scale work for the musical stage. Like

Two future Emperors: Joseph II (right), then co-regent, and Leopold II. Mozart would serve both

the Latin comedy *Apollo et Hyacinthus* K38 which he wrote for Salzburg University two months later, however, it is otherwise distinctive only on account of its composer's tender age. As with other works of Mozart's childhood, it is also difficult to know how large a part Leopold played in the composition; his handwriting certainly appears in the surviving manuscript.

In September 1767 Leopold once again obtained leave of absence from his post, this time to travel with the family to Vienna, where he no doubt hoped to capitalize on celebrations for the forthcoming royal marriage of the Archduchess Maria Josepha to the King of Naples. If so, his plans were thwarted. The bride-to-be succumbed to the smallpox epidemic which would soon be raging in the imperial capital, becoming (as Leopold felicitously puts it) 'the bride of the heavenly Bridegroom' instead. The

Mozart performing at a tea party at Prince Louis-François de Conti's Paris residence, summer 1766

Mozarts fled the infected city for Olmütz in Bohemia, only to find that Wolfgang had already contracted the disease. Nannerl said later that he never really looked healthy thereafter, but for the moment the boy demonstrated once more his remarkable resilience, performing (and complaining about out-of-tune trumpets) in Brno by the end of the year. It was an ill-omened start, though, for what was to be a trip filled with disappointments.

The children appeared again at the Viennese court, but although the Empress's new co-regent, her son Joseph II, would be an important influence on Mozart's later career, nothing came of the visit on this occasion except a vague suggestion that Wolfgang might like to try his hand at an Italian opera. Then, in April, Archbishop Schrattenbach stopped Leopold's salary on the grounds that he had overstayed his leave. In an attempt to salvage something from the situation, Leopold played on the Emperor's hint about an opera to secure a commission for his son from the veteran intriguer and lessee of the two imperial theaters in Vienna, Giuseppe d'Affligio. Wolfgang set to work with a will, completing his first *opera buffa, La finta semplice (The make-believe simpleton)* K51 (*46a*), during the early summer. It was never performed in the capital. Leopold was no stranger to musical intrigue, but he was out of his league with d'Affligio and his Viennese cabals. The only result of his son's labors was a period of frantic politicking and a long, heartfelt petition from Leopold to the Emperor. 'If a man has no talents, he is unhappy enough,' he wrote to Hagenauer on July 30, 1768, 'but if he has, envy pursues him in proportion to his ability.' It was a salutary lesson for the future.

The opera itself, which bears ample witness to the twelve-year-old's proficiency at adapting himself to new and relatively unfamiliar models, only received its first production on the Mozarts' return to Salzburg. In December, however, Wolfgang directed a performance of his *Waisenhausmesse* K139 (47*a*) in the imperial presence to mark the dedication of an orphanage church near Vienna. This is Mozart's first complete mass setting, the most dramatic moment of which comes when the trombones herald the Crucifixus with a doom-laden rhythmic motif (which reappears eighteen years later as a timpani motto in the slow introduction to the 'Prague' symphony). As for opera, Vienna had to content itself with the slender *Singspiel* (literally 'sing-play') *Bastien und Bastienne* K50 (46*b*), a pastoral love story, which was performed privately at the home of Dr. Anton Mesmer of 'animal magnetism' fame. Beethoven later adapted a theme from it for the first subject of his third symphony, the 'Eroica'.

The Mozarts returned to Salzburg on January 5, 1769 and stayed for most of the year, Wolfgang being given the (unpaid) post of Konzertmeister (concertmaster) to the archiepiscopal court in November. The following month he, Leopold and a servant set off on their fifth journey. Their destination this time was Italy, the only major musical center in Europe which had not yet been exposed to Wolfgang's talents at first hand.

ITALY

They arrived in Verona at the end of December and the familiar round of introductions, performances in private and public, and testing of the young Wolfgang began again. In January 1770 they moved on to Mantua where, on the sixteenth, Mozart gave a concert at the Accademia Filarmonica. The program of this concert gives a vivid picture of just how strenuous were his performances. Of the fourteen substantial items listed, nine involved Mozart directly, either as performer or composer or both, and all except two demanded improvisation or sight-reading. He not only played the harpsichord and violin, but also sang while accompanying himself. The program describes him as 'the most highly skilled youth Signor Amadeo Mozart', this journey being the first occasion on which he used a Latinized form of his baptismal name Theophilus.

Mozart's physical appearance at this time is captured in the portrait painted by Saverio dalla Rosa a few days before this concert took place. It seems to bear out Nannerl's claim that he always looked peeky after his smallpox attack, though Leopold at the same time described him as 'fat and cheerful and jolly all day long'.

On January 20 Wolfgang heard Johann Adolf Hasse's *La clemenza di Tito* (which was to be the subject of his own penultimate opera) at Cremona on his way to Milan, where the Mozarts arrived three days later, giving a public concert before continuing to Bologna and Florence. Here he gave a concert before the Grand Duke of Tuscany (later Emperor Leopold II), and met the English child prodigy, Thomas Linley. Linley was exactly his own age and the two boys immediately struck up a friendship. Leopold reports how they performed alternately at the house of a prominent Italian poetess for the whole of one evening, 'constantly embracing each other'. The following day, Linley, who was known in Italy as 'the Tommasino', brought his violin to their rooms and played all afternoon while Wolfgang accompanied him. When the Mozarts left Florence, Linley was inconsolable and insisted on accompanying their carriage as far as the city gates. Charles Burney, the English musical historian, who was also in Florence at this time, wrote that 'the Tommasino . . . and the little Mozart are talked of all over Italy as the most promising geniuses of this age.'

On April 11 the Mozarts arrived in Rome, where Wolfgang gave further proof of his remarkable abilities. Father and son attended the Sistine Chapel to hear Allegri's famous Miserere for double choir, a work closely guarded by the Vatican authorities (though Leopold's claim that the singers were forbidden to take the music away on pain of excommunication is exaggerated). After this single hearing, Wolfgang wrote the whole piece out from memory.

Salzburg in the 1750s; the Archbishop's palace dominated the town's life as well as its skyline

After a six-week sightseeing visit to Naples, where they were received by the prime minister and the British ambassador, William Hamilton (later to be cuckolded by Horatio Nelson), it was back to Rome by the eighteenth-century equivalent of the express train – a mail coach which did the trip in a marathon twenty-seven hours. If the Mozarts required any reminder that travel was a dangerous business, this journey amply provided it. On their way down to Naples they had traveled in convoy because the road was a favorite haunt of bandits. Now, on the way back, their carriage nearly overturned, giving Leopold a nasty leg injury. Before they left for Bologna two weeks later, Wolfgang had had an audience with the Pope and had been presented with the Order of the Golden Spur, the first musician to be so honored since Orlande de Lassus in 1574.

Another honor was to follow in Bologna itself, where Mozart was admitted to the prestigious Accademia Filarmonica after an examination in composition. But more important for his musical development and reputation was the commission for a new opera for the Milan season. He began work on *Mitridate, rè di Ponto* K87 (74*a*) in October and was directing rehearsals by the first week of December. The première took place at the Teatro Regio Ducal in Milan on December 26, with Wolfgang conducting from the harpsichord while Leopold watched nervously from one of the boxes above. Despite its daunting length – some six hours including ballets – it was a resounding success and had a run of twenty-two consecutive performances. After conducting the first three, Wolfgang left for Verona, Turin and Venice, arriving in time for Carnival (and a round of lunch engagements that included most of the upper echelons of Venetian society).

Father and son returned to Salzburg at the end of March 1771, after more than fifteen months away. They stayed at home for less than five months before traveling to Milan again. Mozart had been asked to write another opera, *Ascanio in Alba* K111, this time for the forthcoming wedding celebrations of the Empress's son, Archduke Ferdinand. Once again the work was done at extraordinary speed: Wolfgang only saw the libretto for the first time at the end of August but was already directing the first full rehearsal by the end of September – and this with a heavy cold and cough and under the most distracting conditions. ('Upstairs we have a violinist,' he wrote to

Nannerl, 'downstairs another one, in the next room a singing-master who gives lessons, and in the other room opposite ours an oboist. That is good fun when you are composing! It gives you plenty of ideas.') Less surprising is the postscript he added to one of Leopold's letters on September 21: 'I cannot write much, firstly, because I have nothing to say, and secondly, because my fingers ache so from composing.' The performance, on October 17, was another triumph, Leopold reporting two days later that 'we are constantly addressed in the street by courtiers and other persons who wish to congratulate the young composer.'

The young composer himself was rather more laconic. On November 30, the day when he was received by the Archduke, presumably to be congratulated in person, his postscript to Leopold's letter home reads in its entirety: 'Lest you should think that I am unwell I am sending you these few lines. I kiss Mamma's hand. My greetings to all our good friends. I have seen four rascals hanged here in the Piazza del Duomo. They hang them just as they do in Lyons.'

'LESS OF A MIRACLE'

Despite their obvious successes, the Italian tours mark the end of Mozart's life as a prodigy. He was entering the no-man's land between childhood and adolescence and his years as a *Wunderkind* were numbered. Descriptions such as "little man' begin to appear in the accounts of his appearances and although his powers could still excite amazement and admiration, there are also references to his reputation having been made some time ago when he was, in Charles Burney's words, 'scarcely out of his infant state'. At least one of those who heard him perform in Italy in 1770, the Abbé Ferdinando Galiani, seems to catch himself in the act of not being quite as amazed as he ought to be when he reports the experience to a correspondent: 'I think I wrote to you that little Mosar [sic] is here, and that he is less of a miracle, although he is always the same miracle . . .'.

The letters of recommendation, by which the Mozarts gained access to the great and the good of Europe, seem more than ever part of a courtly dance, of which the steps were the demands of reciprocal duty between one noble household and another and in which Leopold and Wolfgang were merely convenient instruments. For all the genuine astonishment at Wolfgang's precocity, the itinerant Salzburgers are still just 'the musician Mozart' and his performing son, and amazement at Mozart's musicianship almost always occupies less space in these letters than the elaborate professions of gratitude, obedience and desire to be of further service that invariably begin and end them.

More worrying for the prodigy's future was the fact that, behind the expressions of wonder, there lay a marked reluctance to provide more tangible tokens of appreciation. The Empress Maria Theresa herself, who had once granted private audiences to the wonderchild and into whose lap the six-year-old Mozart had leapt with such engaging unselfconsciousness, wrote in no uncertain terms to her son the Archduke when the latter suggested giving the Mozarts a post at his court after he had heard *Ascanio in Alba*:

You ask me to take the young Salzburger into your service. I do not know why, not believing you have need of a composer or of useless people. If however it would give you pleasure, I have no wish to hinder you. What I say is intended only to prevent your burdening yourself with useless people and giving titles to people of that sort. If they are in your service it degrades that service when these people go about the world like beggars. Besides he has a large family [she was misinformed on this point]

Needless to say, the dutiful Archduke thought better of his plan.

On December 15, 1771, the Mozarts, who had presumably been tarrying in Milan to hear the upshot of Ferdinand's deliberations, returned once more to Salzburg. The very next day saw the death of Leopold's employer, the Prince-Archbishop Schrattenbach. It was yet another indication that the old order was changing. Prop by prop, the stage was being set for what were to be perhaps the least rewarding years of Mozart's short life.

In The Service Of The Archbishop

Archbishop Schrattenbach had been a remarkably liberal employer, sanctioning his deputy Kapellmeister's long absences from his post and even continuing to pay his salary during some of his foreign wanderings. No doubt he had an eye to the kudos the young Salzburger's talents reflected on his court, but none the less without his tolerance Wolfgang's international childhood fame could hardly have been achieved.

The new Prince-Archbishop of Salzburg was elected on March 14, 1772. He was Hieronymus, Count Colloredo, the former Bishop of Gurk, who may have served as a witness at the Pope's conferral of the Order of the Golden Spur on Wolfgang less than two years earlier. At the end of April he was installed at Salzburg amid much pomp and ceremony, which probably included a performance of Mozart's *serenata drammatica, Il sogno di Scipione (Scipio's dream)* K126, a one-act theatrical work consisting of an overture and twelve arias on a text by the grand master of *opera seria*, Metastasio.

Colloredo was to play a central role in the development of Mozart's life and career. In the process, he would enter the rogue's gallery of musical history. Whether he was quite the villain that he is often painted, however, is very doubtful. In many respects, at least at the outset, he continued Schrattenbach's policy of generous leniency towards Leopold and Wolfgang, and it is difficult to avoid the conclusion that the irretrievable rift which finally opened between Mozart and his employer was as much the product of the former's increasingly wayward disaffection as of the latter's haughty intransigence.

One of Colloredo's first acts as archbishop, in fact, was to put on a formal footing the position of Konzertmeister that Wolfgang had held on an unpaid basis since 1769. Under the terms of his contract, the sixteen-year-old was to receive 150 gulden a year in return for his services. It was not a bad salary for a young musician, but after almost a decade in the international limelight, during which he had met and been applauded by most of the crowned and ennobled heads of Europe, it must have seemed something of a comedown. Certainly, it would not be long before Mozart was straining at the leash.

KONZERTMEISTER TO COLLOREDO

With Mozart's decade in Colloredo's service we enter a period of relative historical shadow. For much of his extraordinary childhood it is possible to reconstruct Wolfgang's movements – sometimes hour by hour – for days, weeks and even months on end, from Leopold's exhaustive letters home. Now, however, the family were all living in Salzburg and seeing each other and their friends every day; for most of the time there was no longer any need to write. Mozart was to prove as tireless a correspondent as his father when he was away from home, and the journeys he undertook during this time – particularly the disastrous trip to Munich, Mannheim and Paris – come vividly to life under the spotlight of his letters. Of the rest, the daily round of Salzburg life, we can catch only tantalizing glimpses – of shooting matches, visits to friends and relatives, masked balls, fancy dress parties, and of course the continual private and public music making which was the mainstay of the Mozarts' existence wherever they happened to be.

In October 1772, however, after nine months in Salzburg, Leopold and Wolfgang returned to Milan – and hence, briefly, to letter-writing – for the rehearsals and first performance of *Lucio Silla* K135, the opera Mozart had been commissioned to write for the 1772–3 season when he was last there. On the way he also began his first set of six string quartets K155–160, which show a distinctly Italian influence. It was probably only on arrival in Milan that Mozart began work on the opera in earnest, since only then would he have had a chance to familiarize himself with the strengths and weaknesses of the singers. Like other operatic composers of his time, Mozart wrote his arias with specific performers in mind and made a point of 'tailoring' his music (the clothes-making analogy is his own) to their needs and limitations.

The plot of *Lucio Silla*, which turns on the competing claims of love and civic duty amongst the ruling classes of the classical era, is typical of *opera seria*, not least in its convoluted implausibility (though the life of the librettist, a bizarre soldier-turned-poet by the name of Gamerra, runs it a pretty close second: his eccentricities included keeping the exhumed skeleton of a former lover in his house after his marriage!) The music, however, marks a clear advance on that of *Mitridate*. In particular, the Finale to Act I, which opens eerily among the catacombs, is a long and dramatically sustained piece of writing which shows Mozart fully in command of the latest operatic fashions; the arias of the heroine, Giunia, stand out as musical expressions of character as well as technical showpieces; and, perhaps most significant of all for the future, there is a new maturity in the way Mozart uses counterpoint in the final Terzetto of Act II to portray simultaneously the conflicting emotions of the characters involved. It is still a long way from *Le nozze di Figaro (The marriage of Figaro)* K492, but the technique, albeit in embryo, is recognizably the same.

Right: Hieronymous Colloredo, Prince-Archbishop of Salzburg

The road to the première was a predictably bumpy one. There were problems with the singers and large-scale changes to the libretto at the last minute, all of which Wolfgang seems characteristically to have taken in his stride, while Leopold, equally characteristically, fumed and chafed at every setback. Then there was a three-hour delay to the start of the first performance while the Archduke finished writing his New Year greeting letters before going to the theater. As a result, the audience was already restless when the overture struck up, and the opera as a whole didn't finish until two o' clock in the morning. Despite this unpromising start, however, *Lucio Silla* was soon playing to packed houses. The second opera of the season had to be postponed to make way for its twenty-six performances, and Leopold had a diplomatic attack of rheumatism so as to delay their departure from Milan in the hope of picking up a prestigious appointment for Wolfgang.

No such post was forthcoming, and in March 1773 father and son returned home, Wolfgang having in the meantime composed one of the earliest of his works still to find a regular place in the repertoire, the ebullient motet *Exsultate, jubilate* K165 (158*a*) for orchestra and male soprano (written for the castrato Rauzzini, who had sung the part of Cecilio in *Lucio Silla*). Shortly afterwards the Mozarts moved from the apartment in which Wolfgang had been born to the roomier and picturesquely named Dancing Master's House in the Hannibal Platz (now the Makart-platz) on the other side of the river Salzach.

In July, they were off on their travels yet again, this time to Vienna, where they spent much of their time with their friend Dr. Mesmer. If the aim of this visit was to secure a post at court, however, it was another failure. Leopold and Wolfgang were received by the Empress, but – not surprisingly given her dismissive contempt when her son had suggested employing them two years earlier – they came away empty handed. Wolfgang composed his second set of six string quartets K168–173, which are clearly modeled on the recent quartets of the older composer whom Mozart (and posterity) would come to recognize as his only contemporary peer, Joseph Haydn, the brother of the Mozarts' Salzburg colleague Michael. Then, after a few concerts and social calls, they returned to Salzburg around the end of September.

With the exception of a three-month visit to Munich for the first performance of Mozart's opera *La finta giardiniera* K196 in the winter of 1774/5, Wolfgang was to remain in Salzburg for the next four years.

'A PLACE TOO NARROW FOR HIS GENIUS'

Since the age of six the longest period Mozart had spent in Salzburg at any one stretch had been eleven months. He had been away from home for more than two-thirds of the last decade. The life of settled routine was almost completely unfamiliar to him. For the remainder of his days he would show signs of restlessness when there was no prospect of imminent travel, and there is every reason to believe that this new life of enforced immobility quickly began to gall him, especially as Colloredo was proving a far less congenial employer than Schrattenbach.

The stages by which this dissatisfaction set in are unknown, but it is already evident in Leopold's letters home from Milan and by the time Mozart finds his own voice in the letters of 1777 it has reached boiling point. As the former manager of the German theater in Vienna memorably put it in a letter to Leopold in 1778, Salzburg had clearly become 'a place too narrow for his genius'.

So what would Mozart's professional life have been like in the 1770s? Much of what we know of musical life in Salzburg at this time derives from the Mozarts themselves, who can hardly be regarded as an unbiased source. (To take Wolfgang's letters at face value, for example, would be to see the orchestra as a walking embodiment of the seven deadly sins.) No doubt, compared with the more cosmopolitan centers he visited during his travels – Vienna, Paris, Milan – Salzburg was indeed a musical backwater. But it had more than its share of highly skilled musicians, including Leopold himself, Kapellmeister Johann Ernst Eberlin and Michael Haydn, whose compositions the Mozarts respected, even if his drinking and his unsophisticated wife were the frequent butt of their jokes. At the same time, while the court orchestra may not have been able to compare with the one at Mannheim (which was anyway exceptional), the sheer technical difficulty of much of the music Mozart wrote for it and the Salzburg singers – difficulties which make performances of some of his compositions from these years a daunting task even today – testifies to the fact that they were no musical slouches either. The Archbishop himself, contrary to the picture Mozart paints of him as a boorish philistine, was a music lover and a decent violinist.

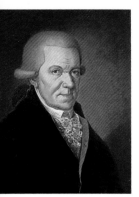

Michael Joseph Haydn, the Mozarts' Salzburg colleague and brother of the more famous Joseph

There were plenty of occasions, too, for Mozart to exercise his performing and compositional skills. The Salzburg orchestra played several times a week and, in stark contrast to modern practice, most of the music it performed would have been newly composed. The university had regular concerts at the end of the academic year

*Musicians
performing
in the
Grand Redoutensaal,
Vienna*

(Finalmusik), and private music making flourished in the homes of the lower nobility and the middle classes. Above all, music played a central part in the life of the court, and maintaining its quality was one of the ways in which the Archbishop – who was also a temporal prince – sought to keep up with the rulers of rival principalities. There was chamber music, music at mealtimes *(Tafelmusik)*, official concerts, and sacred theatrical music (such as Mozart's own *Die Schuldigkeit des ersten Gebots*). The Archbishop's musicians were also responsible for writing and performing church music, of which Mozart composed a great deal during his Salzburg years, including such

enduring works as the 'Coronation' Mass K317 and the *Vesperae solennes de confessore* K339 with its ethereal 'Laudate dominum' for solo soprano and choir. As a devotee of the Enlightenment ideals espoused by Joseph II, Colloredo certainly demanded shorter, less showy sacred works than his predecessors – Mozart complained in one of his letters that no mass was permitted to last more than forty-five minutes – and the orchestra itself did not escape the cutbacks he instituted in some of the more ceremonial aspects of court life. But music was taken seriously (another of Mozart's complaints was in fact that too many people had too much say in what was written and performed) and Salzburg continued to attract talented musicians throughout the period when he was chafing at the bit to seek his fortune elsewhere.

Like his contemporaries, Mozart almost always wrote with a specific occasion in mind (to the extent of abandoning pieces unfinished if the occasion disappeared) and his Salzburg compositions of the 1770s therefore follow the contours of the town's musical life very closely. The vast majority of his church music – not only masses but litanies, vespers, offertories, motets and church sonatas – belongs to this period. So, too, do his violin concertos, probably written for Salzburg virtuosos such as Brunetti, though Mozart, who was a virtuoso violinist (a fact often forgotten because of his reputation as a pianist) also performed them himself; indeed, these five concertos are Mozart's only works in a genre he never touched again once he had left the Archbishop's service.

Also prominent in Wolfgang's output during these years are serenades, divertimentos and cassations, some of them written as *Tafelmusik* for the court, others – such as the famous Haffner serenade of 1776, commissioned for a sister's wedding by Siegmund Haffner, the son of a Salzburg dignitary and businessman – to celebrate significant events in the lives of local families. Others again were written for the university *Finalmusik*, a charming ceremony in which musicians would gather at dusk and process with music to the Mirabell Palace (the Archbishop's summer residence) to perform a serenade; they would then wend their way back across the Salzach bridge for a second performance of the same piece in front of the assembled teachers and students in what is now the Universitätsplatz. Mozart was a popular and frequent choice as composer of these serenades.

The young composer also wrote some twenty-six symphonies during his years in Colloredo's service, most of them in the first two-and-a-half years after Schrattenbach's death. The symphony in the 1770s was far from being the substantial musical form that it became under Beethoven and his successors. It had its roots in the overture and continued to be used as a curtain-raiser for theatrical and sacred works or for concerts, which sometimes began and ended with the opening and final movements of a single work. (Some of Mozart's symphonies from this period were actually adapted to form overtures, or vice versa, and others were reworked from his own serenades.) Mostly festive and charming, with some arresting orchestral effects, the early symphonies from this period are not notably ambitious works, and Leopold himself advised holding them back from publication in case Wolfgang came to think less well of them 'when you are older and have more insight'. None the less, they demonstrate a growing mastery of form, and some, such as the so-called 'Little' G minor K183 (173*d*B) of 1773 and the A major K201 (186) of 1774, presage the expressive range of Mozart's maturity. The mid-1770s seem to have been a relatively fallow period for him as a symphonist, but the works of 1778 to 1780, such as the 'Paris' symphony K297 (300*a*) and the bracing C major K338, recognizably herald the six last great symphonies of Mozart's Vienna years.

Whatever the frustrations and indignities of Mozart's life as a court musician, then, Salzburg was very far from being a musical desert. There were numerous opportunities for him to turn his talents to account in a variety of forms, and if he was treated as a servant this was, after all, the status expected and accepted by the vast majority of the musicians of his time, including the great Joseph Haydn, who spent most of his working life in the livery of the Esterhazy family. Indeed, while Mozart railed against having to take his meals with the Salzburg cooks, he continued, now and for the remainder of his life, to seek employment at other courts, with all the restrictions this would have entailed had he been successful in securing a post. It wasn't the patronage system he found intolerable; it was Salzburg in general and Archbishop Colloredo in particular.

In the light of this and Mozart's increasingly mercurial temperament, tensions were inevitable. On the one hand, his talents were exceptional and he knew it. They required grander scope than the town he was brought up in could provide; above all, he wanted to write operas, for which there was virtually no opportunity there. On the other hand, that very lack of scope contributed to the fact that his absolute self-confidence as a composer, a lifelong and awe-inspiring characteristic, was not yet justified by more than a handful of his works. His superiority to his contemporaries as a performer was proven beyond doubt; his superiority as a composer was never less self-evident than during these years of transition from fêted prodigy to musical maturity. What we can see with hindsight as astonishing self-knowledge must to many in the Salzburg musical establishment, and especially to his employer the Archbishop, have seemed merely the insubordinate arrogance of youth.

LA FINTA GIARDINIERA AND *IL RÈ PASTORE*

If the shortage of opportunities for operatic composition was one of the reasons for Mozart's dissatisfaction at Salzburg, two commissions, in the winter of 1774 and the spring of 1775, provided at least some temporary relief.

The first and most prestigious, for an *opera buffa* called *La finta giardiniera (The make-believe gardener)* came from the superintendant of theatrical entertainments at Munich and derived from the Elector of Bavaria's long-standing interest in Mozart. The work was to be performed as part of the 1774-5 Carnival celebrations and carried the added attraction of travel to the Bavarian capital to direct rehearsals and attend the first performances. With Colloredo's permission, Leopold and Wolfgang set off for Munich on December 6, 1774, Nannerl joining them in January for the much-postponed première on the thirteenth. The opera was a great success, but true to what was by now an all too familiar pattern, led to nothing more permanent in the way of employment, and not even to a commission for the next year's Carnival opera, as Leopold had hoped. In the short term, though, there were masked balls and general applause to sugar the pill, and the Mozarts stayed on to enjoy the rest of the Carnival, only returning to Salzburg in March 1775.

The second commission was an altogether more parochial affair. This was *Il Rè pastore (The shepherd king)* K208, another classical tale of love versus duty, with strong pastoral overtones, which was to form part of the entertainments for the visit to Salzburg in April 1775 of the Archduke Maximilian (the same whose cast-off suit Wolfgang had been given by Maria Theresa thirteen years earlier). The libretto offered little scope for the kind of musical characterization that is a feature of *La finta giardiniera*, and the resulting score, as much as the occasion itself, suggests that Mozart's imagination was not fully engaged.

Thereafter, not only were there no more operatic commissions to fulfill until the decisive one for *Idomeneo* K366 in 1780; there were, until the autumn of 1777, no more opportunities for travel either.

'There is no vacancy here': Munich and Mannheim

The circumstances in which Mozart's journey to Munich, Mannheim and Paris of 1777–9 was undertaken were as explosive as the trip itself was to be disastrous. Relations between the Mozarts and their employer were at a new low and their financial situation had also deteriorated. Again, the details are now lost, but in August 1777 a petition to Colloredo in Wolfgang's name – and couched in extraordinarily tactless, if not actually insolent, terms – requests leave to travel and refers to the Archbishop's refusal to grant previous similar requests. For good measure, Wolfgang (or more likely Leopold on his behalf) takes the liberty of reminding the Archbishop both of what his grace had said on one such previous occasion (namely that Wolfgang had nothing to hope for in Salzburg anyway and had better seek his fortune elsewhere) and, on the other hand, of what the Gospel has to say about the reciprocal duties of parents and talented children. It is perhaps hardly surprising that Colloredo's scribbled response, edited into officialese by his staff before being passed on to the petitioners, was a scathingly dismissive 'Father and son herewith granted permission to seek their fortune according to the Gospel.' Later letters refer to other specific quarrels, but we have only the Mozarts' side of the story.

The dismissal was a bombshell for Leopold, who went into a swift psychosomatic decline, taking to his bed, sick with worry, at the beginning of September. For Wolfgang, on the other hand, it was a heady release.

His optimism might have been dented if he could have seen what lay ahead. As it was, he and his mother set off for Munich on the morning of September 23, 1777 on the first leg of a quest for income – either from commissions or from a permanent appointment – that would keep Wolfgang away from Salzburg for the next sixteen months.

The journey began ominously and got worse. Leopold, fussing over his wife's and son's departure, forgot to give them his paternal blessing and by the time he remembered, their carriage was already out of view beyond the town gates. The oversight threw him and Nannerl into a state of morbid collapse for the rest of the day. Forced to stay behind to make his

Mozart's mother, Anna Maria, in 1775

peace with the Archbishop, the great organizer clearly feared that Wolfgang (who, though nearly twenty-two, had never traveled without him before) still lacked the maturity to make his own way in the world. During his son's absence, he was to send ream upon ream of increasingly anxious fatherly advice on everything from the need for caution when walking on wet cobblestones to the best way of securing influential introductions on arrival in a new town. His doubts were soon to prove justified. The

Mozarts may have fallen into debt since their last journey, but they still had a great deal of musical capital to draw on in the form of goodwill acquired during Wolfgang's childhood tours. It would not be long before Mozart began to squander it.

By waiting on the right people in Munich, he succeeded in arranging an audience with the Elector of Bavaria, Maximilian III Joseph, but one wonders whether his breezy self-confidence might not already have set some teeth on edge. (One of his opening gambits to the supervisor of entertainments at the Bavarian court, for example, was that a first-rate composer was badly needed there.) Mozart sent his father an ostensibly verbatim account of his conversation with the Elector, which was engineered by placing himself in a corridor through which Maximilian had to pass on his way to a pre-hunt mass, and it is perhaps not over-imaginative to detect a certain shrinking on the Elector's part from the urgent gush of Mozart's self-recommendation:

'Your Highness will allow me to throw myself most humbly at your feet and offer you my services.' 'So you have left Salzburg for good?' 'Yes, your Highness, for good.' 'How is that? Have you had a row with him?' 'Not at all, your Highness. I only asked him for permission to travel, which he refused. So I was compelled to take this step, though indeed I had long been intending to clear out. For Salzburg is no place for me, I can tell you.' 'Good Heavens! There's a young man for you! But your father is still in Salzburg?' 'Yes, your Highness. He too throws himself most humbly at your feet. . . . I have been three times to Italy already, I have written three operas, I am a member of the Bologna Academy, where I had to pass a test, at which many maestri have labored and sweated for four or five hours, but which I finished in an hour. Let that be proof that I am competent to serve at any Court. My sole wish, however, is to serve your Highness, who is himself such a great –' 'Yes, my dear boy, but I have no vacancy. I am sorry. If only there were a vacancy –' 'I assure your Highness

that I should not fail to do credit to Munich.' 'I know. But it is no good, for there is no vacancy here.' This he said as he walked away.

So much for Munich. Encouraged by what he claimed in characteristically assured terms to be his great popularity there, and toying with a harebrained scheme whereby a group of acquaintances would club together to subsidize him out of their own pockets, Mozart lingered for another ten days in the hope of commissions or an electoral change of heart. However, it soon became clear that such hopes were vain, and on October 11, he and his mother left for Augsburg, arriving later the same day.

Here his uncle the bookbinder helped Mozart to meet local officials and he gave a public concert wearing his Order of the Golden Spur, an affectation for which he was roundly mocked by the young squirearchy. It was in Augsburg, too, that he got to know his young cousin, Maria Anna Thekla Mozart, better known to posterity as 'the Bäsle'. They immediately found themselves on the same wavelength – 'We two get on extremely well, for, like myself, she is a bit of a scamp. We both laugh at everyone and have great fun' – and Wolfgang later wrote to her the series of infamously scatological letters which have done so much to create the *Amadeus* caricature of Mozart as an embarrassing, giggling child.

Chevalier Mozart:
the twenty-one-year-old
composer wearing the
Order of the Golden Spur

This curious combination of juvenile high spirits and absolute musical seriousness also manifests itself in Mozart's

Top left:
'Like myself, she is a bit of a
scamp': Mozart's cousin,
Maria Anna Thekla Mozart,
the 'Bäsle'

Top right:
The manuscript of one of
Mozart's notorious letters to his
cousin, the Bäsle,
10 May 1779

Bottom:
Another letter to
his cousin, the Bäsle,
5 November 1777

visit to the famous Augsburg piano manufacturer, Stein. Arriving incognito at Stein's shop, he announced himself as Herr Trazom ('Mozart' backwards, one of his favorite pseudonyms), only revealing his true identity through the unmistakable brilliance of his improvisation when he sat down at the keyboard. By contrast, his comments on Stein's pianos, which he greatly admired, are exact, discriminating and professional. He describes in great detail the manufacturing process, the nature of the mechanism and its advantages in terms of sound and touch. It is the tone he applies to all musical matters he considers worth his attention, and contrasts sharply with the inconsequential (if fascinating) gossip of much of the correspondence. Stein reciprocated Mozart's admiration, apparently claiming that no one else had ever got such good results out of his instruments. (The pianos on which Mozart made his name as a performer were fortepianos, and it is for this instrument – one capable of greater flexibility of tone but less volume than a modern concert grand – that most of his keyboard works were written.)

After a farewell concert, mother and son left for Mannheim, then one of the most important musical centers in Germany, where they arrived on October 30. They were to stay for more than four months. Wolfgang immediately showed his usual hypersensitivity to perceived doubts about his talents, when introduced to various musical Mannheimers by the Konzertmeister Christian Cannabich. 'Some who knew me by repute were very polite and fearfully respectful,' he wrote to Leopold; 'others however, who had never heard of me, stared at me wide-eyed, and certainly in a rather sneering manner. They probably think that because I am little and young, nothing great or mature can come out of me; but they will see.' (Interestingly, Leopold too, writing to Wolfgang a few days later, confirms that 'your youth and your appearance prevent people from realizing the wealth of the Divine grace which has been bestowed on you in your talents', and other descriptions of Mozart in his later life also stress his smallness of stature. The Irish tenor Michael Kelly, who knew him in Vienna in the 1780s, described him in his memoirs as 'a remarkably small man, very thin and pale, with a profusion of fine fair hair, of which he was rather vain.')

Despite his usual high-handedness in dismissing the abilities of lesser musicians than himself, Mozart developed a deep respect for the Mannheim orchestra ('this army of generals' as Burney memorably described it), whose discipline and skill he contrasted with the moral and musical laxity of the Salzburg band. At the same time, his own approach to impressing the Mannheim musical establishment was hardly a model of decorum. Secretly taking over the organ at the Elector Palatine's chapel during mass, for example, he played a cadenza after the priest had intoned the Gloria, causing the entire congregation, including Kapellmeister Holzbauer, to look round in amazement. Then, 'in the very best of spirits', he rounded the service off with a couple of improvised fugues!

He succeeded, however, in insinuating himself into court circles, assiduously cultivating the Elector Palatine's natural children as a means to gaining the favor of the Elector himself. Yet again, though, there was no appointment to be had. Furthermore, by the time the Elector got round to confirming the fact, winter had set in, making traveling difficult. To reduce Mozart's prospects still further, the Mannheim court was thrown into confusion and uncertainty at the end of 1777 when the Elector of Bavaria died and the Elector Palatine acceded to the Bavarian electorship in addition to his own, raising questions as to where he would eventually establish his court.

Faced with this dispiriting situation, Mozart drew up plans to travel to Paris with a new friend, the flautist Johann Baptist Wendling, but progress on putting them into effect was painfully slow. In the meantime, he picked up what work he could find,

Barbara Krafft's
posthumous portrait,
generally regarded
as the best likeness
of the composer

taking on pupils and the odd commission. But his heart wasn't in it. Despite claims to his father that he was never really happy unless he was composing, he worked only grudgingly at the set of flute quartets and concertos he was commissioned to write for a local surgeon, failing to complete it (and consequently to get his full fee). While in one form or another music continued to take up most of his time, he was also reveling in his freedom from the hated constraints of Salzburg life.

Meanwhile, Leopold's letters were becoming increasingly frantic. He felt that Wolfgang was spending far too long in Mannheim. This sort of behavior was not going to restore the family finances; on the contrary, it was running them down still further. The first signs of strain in the relationship between father and son begin to appear in the correspondence as Leopold sought urgently to impress on Wolfgang some sense of his responsibilities. 'You must now endeavor to make greater strides', he wrote on January 29, 1778, 'to win for yourself, as far as in you lies, glory, honor, and a great name, and thus make money also. . . .' Later letters are peppered with strictures on his son's unworldliness, his too trusting nature, his addiction to being praised.

By now, however, Wolfgang had another more pressing reason to remain in Mannheim than inclement weather or hopes of a change in his prospects. He had met and fallen in love with Aloysia Weber, the sixteen-year-old daughter of a family that was to play a central role in his future life. Her father, Fridolin Weber, was an impoverished violinist and music copyist (and later uncle to the composer Carl Maria von Weber) and Aloysia herself, one of four daughters, a promising soprano. Out of the blue, at the beginning of February 1778, Leopold received a letter from Wolfgang informing him that he planned to go touring in Italy with the Webers to promote Aloysia as a prima donna. By way of justification, he adds that Wendling, though a thoroughly honest sort, has 'no religion whatever', and traveling to Paris with him would therefore be a blot on Mozart's own reputation. Poor Maria Anna, compliant but obviously worried, secretly appended a note beginning 'You will see from this letter that when Wolfgang makes new acquaintances, he immediately wants to give his life and property for them.'

Leopold reacted with horror. Declaring himself almost prostrate with worry, he stamped on the scheme in no uncertain terms, exhorting his son in words at once furious and moving:

> . . . *it now depends on you alone to raise yourself gradually to a position of eminence, such as no musician has ever obtained. You owe that to the extraordinary talents which you have received from a beneficent God; and now it depends solely on your good sense and your way of life whether you die as an ordinary musician, utterly forgotten by the world, or as a famous Kapellmeister, of whom posterity will read. . . .* Off with you to Paris! *and that soon! Find your place among great people.* Aut Caesar aut nihil.

Wolfgang's disingenuous reply was chilly, defensive and full of wounded innocence. It amounted to a complete climbdown. Four weeks later, on March 14, 1778, he and his mother left Mannheim for Paris. Maria Anna had originally intended to return to Salzburg but, given his conduct in Mannheim, it was clearly felt that Wolfgang could not be trusted on his own. The change of plan was to have tragic consequences for them both.

The Paris fiasco

They arrived in the French capital after a grueling nine-day journey, and put up in dingy lodgings in the rue Bourg l'Abbé. At first all seemed to go well, at least for Wolfgang, who unlike Maria Anna didn't have to sit all day in a room too dark even to knit in. Through the good offices of old friends such as the Baron Grimm, he received some commissions, including the writing of additional choruses, now lost, for a work by Holzbauer. He also presented himself to influential people, though he showed a dangerous lack of patience if he felt he was not being appreciated. When playing before the Duchesse de Chabot, for example, he broke off in the middle of a set of variations when she persisted in playing cards with her friends instead of listening to him. By contrast, when her more appreciative husband arrived, he 'forgot the cold and my headache and in spite of the wretched clavier, I played – as I play when I am in good spirits.'

Equally unlikely to recommend him to Parisian patrons was his robust contempt for French musical taste. 'Let me never hear a Frenchwoman singing Italian arias,' he wrote with typical vehemence in his first letter home. 'I can forgive her if she screeches out her French trash, but not if she ruins good music!' Nor was he any more tactful in his dealings with his fellow musicians than he had been in Mannheim. He could never resist an opportunity to show off his own superior abilities. For example, of the Italian composer Cambini, an influential figure in Parisian musical life, he writes that 'in all innocence I swept the floor with him at our first meeting'.

The Mozarts in Salzburg around 1780: Anna Maria, who had died in 1778, looks down from the wall

Quite how much work Mozart was actually doing it is difficult to know. He certainly had pupils, though he seems to have found teaching tiring and uncongenial and didn't go out of his way to find or keep them. He also scored quite a success with his 'Paris' symphony K297 (300*a*), which was tailored to Parisian taste ('What a fuss the oxen here make of this trick!' he wrote to his father of the loud unison opening) and was performed at the Concert Spirituel – one of the mainstays of the city's musical life – in June. He even claimed to Leopold that he had been offered the post of organist at Versailles and had turned it down. But there is reason to believe that the version of events he gave his father was doctored to put the best gloss on a highly unpromising situation. Even leaving aside Mozart's own shortcomings as a diplomatist, the timing of his visit could hardly have been less propitious: Paris was gripped by a bitter musical controversy as to the respective operatic merits of Gluck and Piccinni and had little time for the young man from Salzburg.

Worse was to follow. In June Mozart's mother fell seriously ill. Baron Grimm's doctor was called, but it was already too late and on July 3, at about 10:20 at night, she died. Mozart wrote two letters immediately afterwards. The first, to his father, warned him that Maria Anna was gravely ill and that, while there was still some hope, she might not recover; in an abrupt change of tone, it then went on to relay various items of musical and social gossip (including, oddly under the circumstances, the fact that 'that godless arch-rascal Voltaire has pegged out, like a dog, like a beast'). The second was to the Mozarts' close Salzburg friend the Abbé Bullinger, to whom he confided the truth, asking him to prepare Leopold to receive the tragic news.

Leopold's next letter makes heart-rending reading. He begins it with best wishes for Maria Anna's approaching name-day, then continues it the next day, by which time he has received Mozart's letter and is in a state of extreme agitation, torn between hope and resignation. The final pages are written later the same afternoon; in the interim Bullinger has taken him aside after one of the shooting matches in which the family and their friends delighted and has gently broken to him the news of his wife's death.

Maria Anna Mozart was buried on July 4, 1778 in the cemetery of Saint-Eustache in Paris. Apart from Wolfgang himself, the only witness was a trumpeter called Heina, whose wife published three of Mozart's piano sonatas. It is perhaps indicative of how few friends Mozart now had in Paris. He was soon to lose another one.

Shortly after his mother's death he moved into the house shared by the Baron Grimm and the latter's mistress, Madame d'Epinay. Relations between Mozart and his new landlord, whose interest in the composer went back to his days as an infant prodigy, soon turned sour. The baron apparently lent Mozart money; Mozart in turn resented his pressure to repay it. Grimm clearly felt that the young man was not temperamentally equipped to make his way in the intrigue-laden world of Parisian music, and there is already a palpable sense of irritation with Mozart's failure to exert himself in the often-quoted letter Grimm wrote to Leopold in Salzburg on July 27: 'He is too trusting, too inactive, too easy to catch, too little intent on the means that may lead to fortune. To make an impression here one has to be artful, enterprising, daring. To make his fortune I wish he had but half his talent and twice as much shrewdness. . . .' By September the friendship had degenerated into open hostility.

In the meantime, Leopold had been active in Salzburg. He, too, evidently despaired of his son's capacity for industrious self-promotion and had decided to take matters into his own hands. On August 31, he wrote to tell Wolfgang that he had persuaded Archbishop Colloredo to offer him his old job back, together with the new responsibilities of court organist, a tripling of his former salary and the opportunity to travel should operatic commissions arise. According to Leopold, Colloredo had even apologized for his past hastiness.

Wolfgang, unimpressed, was in no hurry to take up the Archbishop's offer. It was September 26 before he finally left Paris, traveling by the slow coach via Nancy to Strasbourg. He seems also to have been nervous at the prospect of seeing his father again after what had, by any standard, been a disastrous first foray into the world without him. On October 3 he warned Leopold that, contrary to the impression he had been giving of great musical busy-ness, 'I am not bringing you many compositions because I haven't composed very much.' He lingered in Strasbourg for the whole of October, giving three concerts, all of which were poorly attended and consequently unprofitable. On November 6 he arrived in Mannheim, where he still hoped for an appointment that might save him from a return to Colloredo's service. Despite the ever more insistent promptings of his father, who feared that the Archbishop might change his mind if kept waiting much longer, Wolfgang remained there for more than a month.

It was Christmas Day before he reached Munich, where the Webers were now living, having followed the Mannheim elector there when he acceded to the Bavarian electorship. Here another blow awaited him. Aloysia, his great love, received him coolly, and there was clearly nothing more to be hoped for from her. 'Today I can only weep', he wrote to his father on December 29. On the same day, Mozart's Munich friend Becke also wrote to Leopold, telling him that Wolfgang was 'assailed by some fear lest your reception of him may not be as tender as he wishes' and extolling the young man's childlike honesty and openness. Mozart's fears were well grounded. The day before, Leopold's patience had finally snapped and there was already a letter on its way commanding him to leave for Salzburg at once. 'Your conduct is disgraceful' it read, 'and I am heartily ashamed of having assured everyone that you would quite certainly be home by Christmas or by the New Year at the very latest. Good God! How often have you made a liar of me! . . . I think that I have now made myself quite clear – or am I to take the mailcoach myself and fetch you?'

Even so, Mozart stayed on in Munich until he had presented the electress with his engraved violin sonatas K301–306 and it was January 15, 1779 before he finally arrived back in Salzburg, accompanied – perhaps for protection – by his cousin the Bäsle, whom he had picked up in Augsburg *en route*.

Mozart had been away from home for almost sixteen months. In that time he had secured neither a permanent appointment nor a commission for the grand opera he still burned to write. He had made little or no money to offset the huge expenses of his journey or to help reduce his father's debts. He had failed to extend his reputation as a composer and hence to advance the transition between spectacular childhood fame and the steady adult career upon which his future prospects depended. In the process he had antagonized potential allies and opened the first serious rift between himself and his father. And at the end of it all he remained a servant (albeit a rather better paid one) of the same hated employer in the same hated town as when he had set out.

Whether there was some fundamental flaw in Mozart's personality, or at least in his way of dealing with people, that can explain his repeated failure to find employment commensurate with his talents, we can only guess. Certainly, his letters home during this long journey reveal an often naive personality, trusting and suspicious by turns, with all the high-spirited insouciance of a young man tasting freedom for the first time. They also demonstrate a remarkable facility for rubbing people up the wrong way. It is equally clear, though, that he was able to arouse and give affection easily, and the circle of his friends and acquaintances was always to be an extensive one.

As we have seen, these voluminous letters also reveal some of those less attractive aspects of Mozart's personality which have tended unfairly to dominate the modern, popular perception of him. There is plenty of earthy humor, certainly, with what reads today as an embarrassing emphasis on bodily functions. The letters to the Bäsle are particularly ripe in this respect and were for many years reproduced only in expurgated versions as a result. He also revels in wordplay, rhymes and inversions in a way that might charitably be related to his fascination with musical variations and the stylized repetitions in his treatment of opera libretti, but which remains an uncomfortably childish trait in a young man in his early twenties. The following typical example, from a letter to his cousin of November 13, 1777, combines both characteristics: 'Forgive my wretched writing, but the pen is already worn to a shred, and I've been shitting, so 'tis said, nigh twenty-two years through the same old hole, which is not yet frayed one whit, though I've used it daily to shit, and each time the muck with my teeth I've bit.'

What is not always pointed out, though, is that Mozart shared this kind of humor with both his parents and, according to some contemporary accounts, with a large number of other respectable Salzburgers. Mozart's fifty-six-year-old mother, for example, ends her first letter to her husband from Munich with the unappetizing advice: 'Addio, ben mio. Keep well, my love. Into your mouth your arse you'll shove. I wish you goodnight, my dear, but first shit in your bed and make it burst.'

Even allowing for the breadth of the eighteenth-century conception of humor, however, Mozart was clearly capable of embarrassing his contemporaries. His future brother-in-law Joseph Lange, insightfully contrasting Mozart the musician and Mozart the man, later observed of him: 'Never was Mozart less recognizably a great man in his conversation than when he was busied with an important work. At such time he not only spoke confusedly and disconnectedly, but occasionally made jests of a nature which one did not expect of him, indeed he even deliberately forgot himself in his behavior.' This account is corroborated by one noble lady who disapprovingly described how Mozart (then aged about thirty) improvised magnificently in her presence, only to break off suddenly and begin leaping over tables and chairs meowing like a cat. The contrast between his much commented on immobility at the keyboard and his continual fidgeting when away from it is perhaps another sign that his phenomenal creative concentration required the counterbalance of frequent releases of nervous tension, but one can see how this kind of thing might not have assorted comfortably with Mozart's musical gifts in aristocratic salons.

Much of this is inevitably speculation. What is unquestionable, however, is that, musically, the years 1777–9 saw Mozart's coming of age as a composer. From this period date the first works that have a claim to be counted among his master-pieces: the Piano Concerto K271 in E♭,

Mozart's autograph score of the 'Paris' symphony K297/300a, 1778

major, for example, written in Salzburg in January 1777 for Mlle Jeunehomme; the stormy Piano Sonata in A minor K310 (300*d*), written in Paris in 1778; the 'Paris' symphony. Writing to Leopold from Paris, Mozart had boasted of his undoubted ability to 'more or less adopt or imitate any kind and any style of composition'. If this facility in imitation was at least as much a hindrance as a benefit, it is with the works of these outwardly unsuccessful years that he began to shake it off and to assimilate the numerous influences to which he had been exposed since earliest childhood to the distinctive musical voice we associate with the masterpieces of his maturity.

IDOMENEO

We know little about the period of almost two years between Mozart's return to Salzburg at the beginning of 1779 and his departure for Munich for the rehearsals of his opera *Idomeneo, rè di Creta* K366 in November 1780. Presumably his life returned to the familiar Salzburg pattern, with the familiar Salzburg frustrations. Musically, though, his work had developed greatly since the early 1770s. There is a new richness, a new formal assurance about the major compositions of this period which sets them apart not only from those of Mozart's youth but also from those of his contemporaries.

Shortly after his homecoming, he wrote what is perhaps the greatest of his Salzburg masses, the 'Coronation' Mass, the Agnus Dei of which, for solo soprano and orchestra, prefigures the Countess's aria 'Dove sono' from *Le nozze di Figaro*. Also in 1779 Mozart completed a work begun some years earlier, the incidental music to Gebler's play *Thamos, König in Ägyptum* K345 (336*a*), a relatively little-known set of three choruses and five entr'actes, which is prophetic both of *Die Zauberflöte (The magic flute)* and, in the striking sonorities of the last number for high priest and chorus, of the 'stone guest' scene in *Don Giovanni.*

The same year saw the composition of the sinfonia concertante in E♭ major for violin and viola K364 (320*d*). This work, with its haunting slow movement and its masterful handling of the dialogue both between the soloists and between soloists and orchestra, far transcends its Mannheim models and can claim to be Mozart's finest instrumental work to date. The last of his Salzburg concertos, it looks directly ahead to the masterpieces of his Vienna years.

All these new developments in his music converge in *Idomeneo*. In October 1777, Wolfgang had written to his father, 'I have an inexpressible longing to write another opera. . . . I have only to hear an opera discussed, I have only to sit in a theater, hear the orchestra tuning their instruments – oh, I am quite beside myself at once.' Since the composition of *Il Rè pastore* in 1775, however, the only opportunities for operatic writing had been individual concert arias and two unfinished works, *Semiramis* (now lost, and perhaps not even begun) and *Zaide* K344, a speculative collaboration with the Mozarts' old family friend, the Salzburg court trumpeter Schachtner. It is easy, therefore, to imagine the excitement with which Wolfgang must have received the commission from Elector Karl Theodor in Munich for an *opera seria*.

A sense of excitement pervades the music of this, Mozart's first operatic masterpiece and the crowning work of the *opera seria* tradition. He began it in Salzburg in October before leaving for Munich on November 5 to meet the singers, some of whom he already knew. His letters home from there provide the first detailed insight into

Mozart's working methods as a composer. (Leopold may have had his doubts about his son's ability to run his own life, but he never had the slightest doubt about his abilities as a composer and the correspondence is an exchange of fellow-professionals.) Convinced, contrary to the prevailing view, that the words of an opera should be (as he later put it) 'the obedient daughter of the music', he took the upper hand from the first with his librettist, the Salzburg court chaplain, Abbate Varesco, who complained that he had had to rewrite his text four times as a result. Mozart demanded significant changes to the libretto right up to the last minute, most of them in the interests of greater authenticity or theatrical effect. For example, writing to his father on November 15, 1780, Mozart says:

> *In the last scene of Act II Idomeneo has an aria or rather a sort of cavatina between the choruses. Here it will be* better *to have a mere recitative, well supported by the instruments. For in this scene which will be the finest in the whole opera . . . there will be so much noise and confusion on the stage that an aria at this particular point would cut a poor figure – and moreover there is the thunderstorm, which is not likely to subside during Herr Raaff's {the first Idomeneo's} aria, is it?*

On November 29, he asks Leopold whether he doesn't think the speech of the subterranean voice – the climactic point in Act III of the opera – is too long to be effective:

> *Consider it carefully. Picture to yourself the theater, and remember that the voice must be terrifying – must penetrate – that the audience must believe that it really exists. Well, how can this effect be produced if the speech is too long, for in this case the listeners will become more and more convinced that it means nothing.*

'The most charming
and lovable lady':
Mozart's patroness
Maria Wilhelmine,
Countess Thun

Such passages reveal Mozart as highly attuned to the theatrical possibilities of his art and are ample proof that, whatever his attributes as a social animal, he was always thoroughly serious and self-conscious as a musician. Other asides bear witness to one of Mozart's most phenomenal attributes as a composer, namely his astonishing powers of concentration. Speaking of the final stages of the opera, he tells Leopold, 'Everything has been composed, but not yet written down', and this distinction between 'composing' and 'writing down' was one that he would make for the rest of his life. Sending a prelude and fugue for piano to his sister shortly after his move to Vienna, for example, he apologized for the fact that in the manuscript the fugue came first and the prelude second, explaining that he composed the fugue first and wrote it out while he was composing the prelude – a degree of mental organization little short of superhuman.

Much of December 1780 was taken up with rehearsals for the opera. In January 1781 visitors, including Leopold and Nannerl, began to arrive in Munich from Salzburg for the first performance (the opera was very much a Salzburg affair, the composer, librettist and translator all being Salzburg citizens). The première, which took place in the Court Theater on January 29, after a week's delay, was a tremendous success and there were two repeat performances. The freshness and originality of the music were widely noticed. Indeed, there is about *Idomeneo* an urgency, an almost breathless verve, that distinguishes it from the later, greater operas. It is the music of a young man relishing the exercise of an imagination too long denied an outlet.

Mozart was coming into his prime. But the triumph of *Idomeneo* must have been a further reminder of how limited the scope was for exercising his powers at Salzburg compared with the opportunities offered by the more cosmopolitan musical centers of Europe. It would not be long before matters came dramatically to a climax.

The break with the Archbishop

Flushed with the success of his opera, Mozart stayed on in Munich with his family for more than a month after the first performance. Archbishop Colloredo, meanwhile, had moved with his retinue to Vienna to attend his ailing father. On March 12, 1781, Colloredo ordered Mozart, who had already outstayed his official leave, to join him there.

Mozart arrived in Vienna alone on March 16, taking up quarters with the archiepiscopal entourage in the House of the Order of Teutonic Knights, and was required to take part in a concert the same day. From being the toast of the town in Munich, he was suddenly a servant again, at Colloredo's beck and call. Like all court musicians, he had to take his meals with the other servants, though as he wrote acerbicly to his father, 'At least I have the

The Emperor Joseph II in 1785

honor to be placed above the cooks.' This status was particularly galling since Mozart already had acquaintances among the Viennese nobility with whom he was meeting regularly on more or less equal terms. The two worlds in which he was used to moving – the small one of the Salzburg court and the wider one of the musically informed nobility – had suddenly collided. Worse still, Colloredo acted, as Wolfgang wrote to Leopold, 'as a *screen* to keep me from the notice of others'. Anxious to attract the

attention of the new Emperor Joseph II (who had been co-regent with his mother, Maria Theresa, until the latter's death at the end of 1780), Mozart found himself instead tied up with private concerts to entertain the Archbishop and his sick father. His frustration knew no bounds when, on April 8, such a concert forced him to forgo a performance in the salon of his well-connected friend and patroness Countess Thun at which Joseph II was present and gave all the players a gift of fifty ducats – about half Mozart's annual salary.

It was only a matter of time before this frustration boiled over. 'We have always been utterly different *in every way* from the other court musicians', Wolfgang wrote to his father in April, and his behavior seemed calculated to highlight that difference in the most conspicuous manner. For example, arriving for a concert at the house of Prince Galitzin, the Russian ambassador and later one of Mozart's principal patrons, he found a servant waiting to show him in but

The Emperor Joseph II in formal court dress

I took no notice, either of the valet or the lackey, but walked straight on through the rooms into the music room, for all the doors were open, – and went straight up to the Prince, paid him my respects and stood there talking to him. I had completely forgotten my friends Ceccarelli and Brunetti, for they were not to be seen. They were leaning against the wall behind the orchestra, not daring to come forward a single step.

Mozart, only too aware of the opportunities Vienna could offer to a person of his talents, was moving inexorably towards a break with Colloredo, his growing recklessness reflected in the progressive abandonment in his letters home of the cypher the family always used in correspondence they thought might cause trouble with the Salzburg censor. At the beginning of May he moved out of the archiepiscopal accommodation into a house known rather sinisterly as The Eye of God, and one can only imagine Leopold's reaction on learning that his son's new landlady was Madame Weber, now a widow, who had moved to Vienna in 1779 and was living there with three of her daughters (the fourth, Mozart's former love Aloysia, having married the actor Joseph Lange in the interim).

On May 9 Mozart was summoned to an interview with the Archbishop at which, if Mozart's own account is to be believed, Colloredo roundly abused him for declining to return to Salzburg immediately as he had been bidden to do and showed him the door, proclaiming that he would have nothing further to do with him. Mozart, rather late in the day, said as he left the room, 'This is final. You shall have it tomorrow in writing.' He spent the next month cultivating his Viennese acquaintances and trying to get the Archbishop's secretariat to accept his formal memorandum of resignation (which they never did), while writing self-justificatory letters to his father who, though his side of the correspondence is lost, was clearly appalled at the turn of events and deeply concerned for both his own and his son's future.

On June 8, 1781, Mozart had his last interview with the Archbishop's chief steward, Count Arco, at which the latter, perhaps frustrated at the young composer's intransigent refusal to be conciliated – his previous attempts to persuade him to stay included a prophetic warning about the fickleness of Viennese taste – finally dismissed him 'with a kick on the arse'.

With that kick Mozart's decade in the service of Archbishop Colloredo came to an end. He would see Salzburg only once more before his death.

Freelance in Vienna

'This is a splendid place,' Mozart had written to his father from Vienna in April, 'and for my métier the best in the world.'

A month and a dismissal later he was still irrepressibly optimistic: 'My luck is just beginning', he wrote after his concluding interview with Colloredo; and a few days later, 'I have the finest and most useful acquaintances in the world. I am liked and respected by the greatest families. All possible honor is shown to me and I am paid into the bargain . . . I pledge myself to succeed.'

The fashionable Graben, Vienna: the Mozarts lived in the Trattnerhof (right foreground) in 1784

Vienna in 1781 must certainly have seemed a promising place for a man of Mozart's talents and temperament. It was the cosmopolitan hub of a huge empire and had a correspondingly lively cultural life, especially in comparison with provincial Salzburg. It was a magnet for musicians from throughout the Habsburg territories and beyond. The presence in the city and its environs of the leading aristocratic and noble families provided ample opportunities for patronage and a ready supply of pupils prepared to pay handsomely for a grounding in music. There were two imperial theaters – the Burgtheater and the Kärntnertortheater – and the Emperor Joseph II, now embarking in earnest on his controversial program of Enlightenment reforms, had committed himself to the promotion of German opera. Furthermore, there was a flourishing private and public concert circuit. Above all, as Mozart – the greatest keyboard virtuoso of his time – was quick to point out to his anxious father, Vienna was 'the land of the clavier'.

The Schönbrunn Palace, Vienna

At the same time, Mozart had launched himself on unfamiliar waters. There was no tradition of self-employment for composers in the eighteenth century, and few freelance performers could rely on commanding significant fees. Viennese taste was notoriously fickle, as Count Arco had warned, and the very concentration of musicians in the capital made it a hotbed of self-interest and intrigue. Furthermore, Mozart's previous attempts to set himself up away from Salzburg hardly gave grounds for optimism. Then he had at least had the Archbishop's payroll to fall back on. Now, his Salzburg bridges well and truly burnt, he was on his own in an alien city with no guaranteed means of support whatsoever.

DIE ENTFÜHRUNG AUS DEM SERAIL

Over the following months he set about establishing himself in Vienna. Urging his father to put the 'accursed affair' of his dismissal behind him, he sent home for the scores of keyboard, instrumental and choral works with which he hoped to impress his new public, as well as for such accoutrements of urban living as presentable clothes and a walking stick. He remained sanguine about his prospects, but repeatedly failed to send Leopold the sum of money he had promised him as a token of his earning power. It was the worst time of year for introducing himself to the leading families, most of them being out of town for the summer, but he acquired a handful of pupils, including the female cousin of Count Cobenzl, on whose beautiful country estate outside Vienna he stayed for much of July, and Josepha von Auernhammer, to whom (despite being rude about her appearance in his letters) he dedicated various keyboard sonatas. These teaching fees were a small but necessary income.

Then, at the end of July, the actor and playwright Gottlieb Stephanie gave Mozart the libretto of what was to become the *Singspiel, Die Entführung aus dem Serail (The abduction from the harem)* K384. This slight tale of the attempted rescue of two captive women from a harem by their lovers, and the magnanimity of the Pasha in forgiving the perpetrators, clearly ignited Mozart's imagination. The story was similar to that of his unfinished opera *Zaide*, the score of which he had brought with him from Munich, and catered to the current Viennese craze for all things Turkish. Despite his avowed intention to write nothing for which there was no prospect of performance (and therefore payment), Mozart was determined to attract the Emperor's attention, and could see the benefit of having an opera in preparation that could be played, if Joseph so wished, during a projected visit by the Grand Duke Paul of Russia in September. Within two days of receiving the libretto, he had already composed an aria for the heroine (Constanze) and the hero (Belmonte) and a trio to end Act I. The first act was completed by the end of August, but as the prospect of performance then receded, Mozart's rate of composition also slowed. Acts II and III were not completed until May 1782, less than two months before the long-delayed première in July.

Mozart approached the composition of *Die Entführung* with even more self-confidence than he had shown in writing *Idomeneo*. Stephanie was treated as a junior partner in exactly the same way as Varesco had been, Mozart explaining what he was looking for in particular arias and even completing the music of one of them before the poet had written the words. He also demonstrated again his instinct for what would work in the theater and the musical means to achieve it. In September 1781, for example, he wrote to his father about the aria in Act I in which Osmin, the overseer of the harem, vents his anger against the would-be rescuer Pedrillo. The passage not only gives an insight into Mozart's creative processes, but also reveals his highly conscious, calculating approach to theatrical music as a medium of expression:

As Osmin's rage gradually increases, there comes (just when the aria seems to be at an end) the allegro assai, which is in a totally different meter and in a different key; this is bound to be very effective. For just as a man in such a towering rage oversteps all the bounds of order, moderation and propriety and completely forgets himself, so must the music too forget itself. But since passions, whether violent or not, must never be expressed to the point of exciting disgust, and as music, even in the most terrible situations, must never offend the ear, but must please the listener, or in other words must never cease to be music, *so I have chosen a key foreign to F (in which the aria is written) but one related to it – not the nearest, D minor, but the more remote A minor.*

The autograph score of
Belmonte's first aria from
Die Entführung aus dem Serail

Equally calculated was the effect Mozart intended the opera to have on his career. 'If it is [a success],' he wrote home, 'then I shall be as popular in Vienna as a composer as I am on the clavier.'

It was. *Die Entführung* 'surpassed public expectation', according to the *Magazin der Musik*, 'and the delicate taste and novelty of the work were so enchanting as to call forth loud and general applause.' The Emperor is said to have congratulated the composer, albeit with the equivocal words 'Too beautiful for our ears, and a prodigious lot of notes,' to which Mozart is supposed to have replied 'Just as many notes, your Majesty, as are necessary.' Whether or not this suspiciously neat exchange ever took place, *Die Entführung* was to remain the most popular of Mozart's operas in his lifetime, and was frequently performed in cities throughout Germany in the 1780s.

THE OTHER CONSTANZE

In the meantime, momentous events had been taking place in Mozart's private life. As early as July 1781, rumors had reached Leopold in Salzburg of a liaison between Mozart and one of his landlady's daughters, Constanze Weber, the nineteen-year-old younger sister of Aloysia. Mozart dismissed them as 'silly talk' based solely on the fact that they were living in the same house, and inveighed against marriage in terms rather too emphatic to be convincing. He admitted, though, that the rumors had been circulating in Vienna too, and that he had considered leaving the Webers' house to quiet them. At the end of August he did so, though only to a furnished room in the same neighborhood

However, while he was working on *Die Entführung* – whose heroine, as we have seen, was also called Constanze – the relationship seems to have deepened and in December, despite his earlier protestations, Mozart wrote to his father telling him of his plans to marry. His stated reasons were no more flattering to Constanze than his description of her physical appearance ('She is not ugly but at the same time far from beautiful', a claim that appears to be born out by her brother-in-law Joseph Lange's portrait). He wanted, he said, someone to look after his domestic needs and an outlet for 'the voice of nature', given that he had 'too much horror and disgust, too much dread and fear of diseases . . . to fool about with whores' and too much religion and honor to 'seduce an innocent girl'. In fact, Mozart had allowed himself to be maneuvered by Constanze's guardian into signing an official document guaranteeing either to marry her within three years or to pay her a substantial yearly sum for life. He claimed that such an agreement was easy for him to enter into, given his affection for Constanze, and that she anyway tore up the document as soon as her guardian left, but one can understand Leopold's reluctance to give his blessing to the proposed union on these terms.

On August 4, 1782, after an enigmatic crisis during which Mozart feared that Madame Weber would have Constanze fetched from his house by the police, they were married in St. Stephen's Cathedral. (Leopold's blessing only arrived by a subsequent post.) According to Mozart, the witnesses were deeply moved by the couple's evident emotion.

Constanze Mozart has generally received a bad press from music historians, not least because Leopold's and Nannerl's unfavorable reactions to her have colored what little we know about her life with the composer. In fact, there are few grounds for thinking her the flighty creature of legend, whose shallow improvidence helped drive her unworldly husband into debt and an early grave; nor is there any evidence to suggest that she failed to appreciate his talents. She came from a musical family and was herself a creditable singer with a taste for that most intellectual of musical forms, the fugue. After Mozart's death she organized her own financial affairs with some aplomb, promoted her husband's music widely, and exercised an unusual degree of editorial care in making his manuscripts available to music publishers. Posterity also owes her a debt of gratitude for the remarkable dedication and broad-mindedness with which she made letters, documents and personal reminiscences available to early biographers, including

Constanze Mozart in 1782, by her brother-in-law Joseph Lange

her own second husband, Georg Nikolaus Nissen. Constanze's illnesses – an expensive business in the days before the welfare state – no doubt contributed to the Mozarts' failure to live within their means, but as for extravagance and irresponsibility, it is at least as fair to say that Mozart's early years provide more examples of both than Constanze's later ones.

Whatever the truth, the marriage appears to have been a very happy one. Mozart's surviving letters to his wife are intimate, affectionate and protective, and show him restless, unhappy and slow to compose when separated from her. Hers to him no longer survive, but there is no reason to doubt that she reciprocated his feelings. She was certainly devastated by his death – to the extent of trying to contract his fatal illness in the first transport of her grief – and she devoted much of her remaining life to the preservation of his memory.

Early success

Mozart's first years as a freelance in Vienna amply justified the hopes of success that he had entertained during his last days in Colloredo's service. In the summer of 1781 he had told Leopold that he would reconsider his position in the winter, with a view to leaving Vienna for Paris if he had not found sufficient work there by then, and again in the summer of 1782 he took to practicing his French and English, presumably with thoughts of a foreign appointment in mind. In the event, though, except for a few brief trips to nearby musical centers, he was to spend the rest of his life in the imperial capital.

His acquaintances among the Viennese nobility seem to have been as numerous and supportive as he had claimed when writing to his father in 1781. He also quickly gained the respect of the Emperor, who played host to the famous musical duel between Mozart and the Italian-born virtuoso and composer Muzio Clementi in December 1781 and was still effusive on the subject when the diarist Count Zinzendorf met him a year later. (After the contest Mozart characteristically dismissed Clementi as 'a mere *mechanicus*', while Clementi's verdict on his rival was far more generous.) Despite such tokens of

'*A mere* mechanicus'?
The pianist and composer Muzio Clementi

imperial favor, however, there was still no offer of a post at court, and Mozart continued to be entirely reliant for his income on teaching, commissions, concert-giving and publication.

The pace of his life became frenetic as he sought to accommodate all these demands on his time. Scarcely was the first performance of *Die Entführung* over, for example, than he set about arranging the opera for wind band in order to earn some additional income from it (and to forestall other arrangers, who, in the absence of copyright restrictions, were apt to descend on a successful score like vultures). While he was doing so – and planning both his marriage and one of the many changes of address that punctuate his Vienna years – his father wrote asking him to compose a new symphony for the celebrations of his friend Haffner's ennoblement. He set to work with a will, sending the music in installments over the next few days (while also composing a new wind serenade), and was astonished when he saw the score again the following year, claiming to have forgotten every note of what is now one of his best-known symphonies (the 'Haffner', K385). There were private and public concerts to be given, for many of which he wrote new works for himself, his friends or his pupils to perform, as well as continuing to astonish audiences with his improvisations; and there were new musical influences to be assimilated – most notably the works of J. S. Bach and Handel, which Mozart got to know at the house of his influential friend, patron and fellow musician, the imperial censor Baron Gottfried van Swieten, and which left an indelible mark on the contrapuntal texture of his own compositions. In addition, the Mozarts conducted an active (and no doubt expensive) social life, which included an all-night ball at their apartment in January 1783 and the performance of a masquerade at a carnival ball in the Redoutensaal the following March. In the light of all this activity, it is perhaps not surprising that Mozart's letters home become shorter and less frequent as the months go by or that the household seems already to have fallen into periodic debt.

The Mozarts' first child, Raimund Leopold, was born on June 17, 1783 (Constanze later said that Mozart had incorporated her labor cries into the D minor string quartet K421 (417*b*) which he was writing at the time). The following month they left the baby with a wet nurse and set off for a long-postponed visit to Salzburg. Little is known about their three-month stay – the last time Mozart would see the town of his birth – but this first meeting with Constanze seems not fully to have dispelled Leopold's doubts about the wisdom of his son's marriage. The day before they left Salzburg at the end of October, Mozart directed the first performance of a work apparently begun (but never finished) as an act of thanksgiving for that marriage – the C minor

Mozart's friend and patron,
the Imperial Censor
Baron Gottfried van Swieten

Mass K427 (417*a*) – in the church of St. Peter's Abbey, Constanze probably taking one of the solo soprano parts. On their way back to Vienna, the couple stayed in Linz with the father of their Vienna friend Count Thun. Here, between October 13, and November 4, Mozart wrote a new symphony 'at breakneck speed' for performance during their visit. This was the magnificent 'Linz' symphony K425, the highly unusual use of trumpets and drums in the slow movement of which was to influence Beethoven in the slow movement of his own first symphony. It may only have been on their return to Vienna at the end of November that the Mozarts discovered their son had died while they were away (on August 19). The only mention of the event in Mozart's surviving correspondence is a single sentence at the end of a letter to Leopold which is otherwise concerned entirely with opera.

The whirl of activity continued into 1784. Mozart was working on another opera, *L'oca del Cairo* K422, which was never completed (and consequently never entered into the thematic catalog of his works that he began to keep in February of this year and maintained meticulously until his death). He was also much in demand as a performer, as can be seen from his heavy schedule for the Lent season: between February 26 and April 1 he gave nineteen concerts, including three by subscription in a private hall in his new lodgings, the Trattnerhof. The list of subscribers for the latter contains a staggering 176 names from among the great and good of Viennese society – more than

Mozart's two surviving children,
Karl Thomas (right) and Franz Xaver Wolfgang, about 1798

the combined lists of his two nearest rivals, Richter and Fischer. At the last of these Lenten concerts, in the Burgtheater, the program included the first performance of the quintet for piano and wind K452, which Mozart described to his father as 'the best work I have ever composed'.

In August 1784 Mozart's sister married the magistrate Johann Baptist von Berchtold zu Sonnenburg, who held the office her own maternal grandfather had held, and left Salzburg to live in the same house in St. Gilgen in which her mother had been born. In Vienna the following

*Mozart's sister
Nannerl in 1785,
as the wife of
Johann Baptist Franz
von Berchtold zu Sonnenburg*

month, Mozart and Constanze moved to a grander and more expensive apartment in the fashionable Domgasse, the annual rent on which was more than his entire Salzburg salary had been. A week earlier Constanze had given birth to another son, Karl Thomas, one of only two of their six children to survive early childhood. He was to outlive both his parents, dying as a junior government official in Milan in 1858.

MOZART AND THE FREEMASONS

In December 1784 Mozart joined the Viennese masonic lodge *Zur Wohlthätigkeit* (Beneficence), senior members of which he had known for some time. Mozart's association with the freemasons has been the subject of much sensational speculation, none of which has any foundation in fact. Secret and ritualistic though the Vienna lodges were, they were far from being the sinister organizations of legend. In fact, *Zur Wohlthätigkeit*, later subsumed into *Zur neugekrönten Hoffnung* (New-crowned Hope), was dedicated to much the same rationalist ideals as informed Joseph II's reforms. (Indeed, many high-ranking government officials were masons.) It was a meeting point for like-minded writers, artists and thinkers from a wide range of social classes. That membership was quite compatible with orthodox religious belief is shown by the fact that Leopold Mozart, a devout Catholic, was admitted to the brotherhood when he stayed with his son in Vienna in 1785.

There is no doubt that Mozart took his freemasonry seriously. He advanced swiftly through the orders, becoming a master mason in January 1785. He also composed a number of works specifically for masonic occasions, and masonic associations have been found, with varying degrees of plausibility, in many of his other compositions, including the overtly masonic *Die Zauberflöte*. He regularly visited other lodges in Vienna and elsewhere, including *Zur wahren Eintracht* (True Harmony) of which his friend Joseph Haydn was at one time a member, and continued to take part in masonic activities even after December 1785 when Joseph II's controversial Freemasonry Act imposed severe restrictions on the lodges. In fact, he remained an active member of *Zur neugekrönten Hoffnung* until his death (with which there is not the slightest evidence that the masons were connected). His last public appearance was at a meeting of the lodge in November 1791.

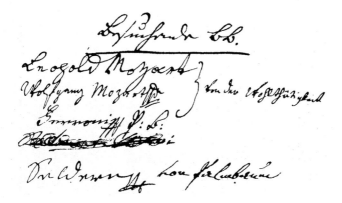

Leopold and Wolfgang Mozart's signatures from a 1785 protocol of the 'Zur wahren Eintracht' lodge

A Viennese masonic lodge meeting, c. 1790: the seated figure far right is almost certainly Mozart

'THE GREATEST COMPOSER KNOWN TO ME'

In February 1785 Leopold Mozart had the opportunity to judge the extent of his son's success at first hand, when he arrived in Vienna for a ten-week visit. His stay coincided with the peak of Mozart's popularity, and Leopold's letters to Nannerl paint a vivid picture of his son's life at this period. The very evening of Leopold's arrival, Mozart gave the first of six Friday concerts at the Mehlgrube casino in the Neue Markt, at which he performed his new D minor piano concerto K466, a work of brooding drama often seen as a precursor of nineteenth-century Romanticism. The following evening there was a quartet party in Mozart's apartment, at which Joseph Haydn was present and heard the last three string quartets (K458, 464 and 465) of the set of six Mozart dedicated to him (he had heard the first three – K387, 421 and 428 – in January). Afterwards, the older composer remarked to Leopold: 'Before God and as an honest man, I tell you that your son is the greatest composer known to me either in person or by name. He has taste and, what is more, the most profound knowledge of composition.' It was a moving tribute from one of the two

The Neue Markt (Mehlmarkt), Vienna: Mozart often gave concerts in the Casino here

greatest living composers to the other and one repaid by Mozart himself in the unconventionally heartfelt dedicatory letter to the published score of his 'Haydn' quartets.

The very next evening, Leopold was present at his son's concert in the Burgtheater and was moved to tears by the 'glorious concerto' he played (perhaps K456 in B♭ major). Joseph II, who was also present, waved his hat and shouted 'Bravo, Mozart!' when the composer left the platform.

Leopold, now (by eighteenth-century standards) an old man of sixty-five, was clearly a little overwhelmed by Mozart's glittering lifestyle, his luxurious apartment and the ferment of musical activity in which he lived, writing wearily to Nannerl on March 12:

We never get to bed before one o'clock and I never get up before nine. We lunch at two or half past. The weather is horrible. Every day there are concerts; and the whole time is given up to teaching, music, composing and so forth. I feel rather out of it all. . . . It is impossible for me to describe the rush and bustle. Since my arrival your brother's fortepiano has been taken at least a dozen times to the theater or to some other house.

In addition, there were numerous social calls to be made. All in all, despite the great respect in which he was evidently held by Mozart's musical circle, Leopold was no doubt somewhat relieved to return to the relative tranquillity of Salzburg at the end of April. Mozart and Constanze accompanied him as far as Purkersdorf a few miles from Vienna before saying their goodbyes. It was the last time father and son would see each other.

In the light of all this 'rush and bustle' it is to be wondered how Mozart found time to compose at all, let alone to write the masterpieces that flowed from his pen during these early Vienna years. He was working at the height of his powers, breaking new ground in almost every major form he touched and accomplishing in the process an unprecedented fusion of the *galant* and learned styles. His comment to Leopold on the three piano concertos K413, 414 and 415, written around the end of 1782, is illuminating in this respect:

> *These concertos are a happy medium between what is too easy and too difficult; they are very brilliant, pleasing to the ear, and natural, without being vapid. There are passages here and there from which the connoisseurs alone can derive satisfaction; but these passages are written in such a way that the less learned cannot fail to be pleased, though without knowing why.*

These and the twelve great piano concertos he wrote for his own and others' performance between 1784 and 1786 mark the most significant development in the history of the concerto form, with symphonic, chamber and operatic elements converging in a perfectly balanced dialogue between soloist and orchestra. The diversity of these concertos is astonishing – far greater, for example, than that of Beethoven's piano concertos – ranging from the buffa grace of K453 in G major to the tragic drama of K491 in C minor (of which Beethoven was later to exclaim 'We shall never be able to do anything like that!') In no sphere other than opera was Mozart's contribution to be so revolutionary.

The two symphonies he wrote during this period, the 'Haffner' and the 'Linz', not only betray no sign of the extreme haste in which they were composed; both also firmly belong to the canon of his mature masterpieces.

Mozart wrote fewer serenades in Vienna than in Salzburg, since there were fewer occasions for them; but such pieces as the wind serenades in E♭ major K375 and C minor K388 (384*a*) reveal a tautness and emotional depth absent in even the most ambitious of his previous works in the form and fully exploit the vibrant Viennese *Harmonie* (wind band) tradition which was also to leave its mark on Mozart's orchestral writing. The magical sonorities of the Gran Partita for thirteen instruments K361 (370*a*), which may have been Mozart's wedding present to Constanze, mark perhaps the highest achievement of the eighteenth-century serenade tradition.

Mozart's work during his first half-decade in Vienna greatly influenced the development of chamber music too. We have already noted Mozart's opinion of his own quintet for piano, oboe, clarinet, horn and bassoon K452, probably the first as well as the greatest work to face the textural challenges of this unusual combination of

instruments. Equally mould-breaking were his two fine quartets for piano and strings, in G minor K478 and E♭ major K493; indeed, the publisher Hoffmeister declined to take any more of them unless Mozart wrote 'more popularly' – an ominous hint that some at least of his music was already becoming too rarefied for a non-professional audience. The finest chamber works of these years, however, are the six string quartets dedicated to Joseph Haydn. The 'fruit of long and laborious endeavour', as Mozart described them in his dedication, they occupied him from 1783 to 1785 and the many surviving sketches and alterations in the autograph scores serve to prove that his legendary facility in composition is only half the

Joseph Haydn

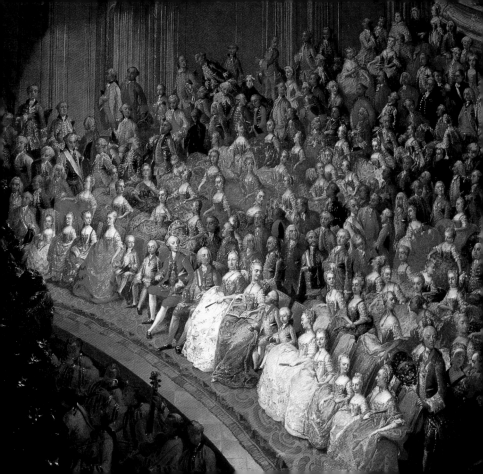

story. Building on Haydn's own achievements in the form, these are quartets in which the four voices contribute as equals to a rich and perfectly balanced conversation. Now recognized as among the greatest quartets ever written, their chromaticism, closely worked counterpoint and adventurous harmonic progressions proved incomprehensible to some contemporary critics. One effectively accused Mozart of writing twelve-tone music, while another gentleman amateur tore the first page of the famous 'Dissonance' quartet (K465) from the score and stamped on it, complaining that the parts were wrongly printed. 'It is a pity,' the *Magazin der Musik* opened in 1786, 'that in his truly artistic and beautiful compositions Mozart should carry his effort after originality too far, to the detriment of the sentiment and heart of his works. His new quartets . . . are much too highly spiced to be palatable for any length of time.'

But these were as yet dissenting voices. More representative was the visitor from Vienna who reported to Leopold in November 1785 that 'in all the announcements of musical works I see nothing but Mozart' and that publishers of the quartets in Berlin 'merely add the following words: "It is quite unnecessary to recommend these quartets to the public. Suffice it to say that they are the work of Herr Mozart".' Leopold, writing to his daughter, grumpily adds that he could say nothing, not having had a letter from his son for more than six weeks. 'My informant', he continued, 'said something too about a new opera. Basta! I daresay we shall hear about it.'

This testy aside is the first recorded mention of *Le nozze di Figaro*, the work that was to be the jewel in the crown of Mozart's first half-decade in Vienna.

Previous page: A gathering in the Grand Redoutensaal, one of the hubs of Viennese social life in the 1780s

Le nozze di Figaro

Mozart had been itching to write another opera ever since he finished *Die Entführung* in 1782. In a letter to his father the following May, he claimed to have read more than a hundred librettos without having found one suitable to his needs. The collaboration on *L'oca del Cairo* with his *Idomeneo* librettist, Varesco, had come to nothing, and another projected opera, *Lo sposo deluso*, had also proved abortive, since when he had had to make do with writing arias for insertion into other people's operas. In February 1786 he wrote the short *Singspiel, Der Schauspieldirektor (The impresario)* K486 for performance – together with a work by the court Kapellmeister, Antonio Salieri – in the orangery at Schönbrunn Palace during a banquet to celebrate a visit by Joseph II's brother-in-law the Governor-General of the Austrian Netherlands; and in March he revised *Idomeneo* for a one-off revival at Prince Auersperg's. But by then he had already found the libretto he had been looking for and had begun the creative collaboration with the Italian poet Lorenzo da Ponte that was to produce his three greatest *opera buffe*.

Lorenzo da Ponte, libertine and librettist

The choice of the story of Figaro's wedding was in some ways an obvious one and in other ways highly controversial: obvious because the play on which it was based, Beaumarchais' *La folle journée ou Le mariage de Figaro*, was the sequel to *Le barbier de Séville*, Paisiello's operatic version of which had been an unprecedented popular success in Vienna; controversial because performance of the play, with its revolutionary undertones, had recently been banned by Joseph II in the imperial capital.

Lorenzo da Ponte, though, was not a man to be put off by a matter like that. Poet, libertine, adventurer, his colorful career had already encompassed a spell as a priest, various scandalous sexual intrigues, a charge of inciting young people to heresy and sedition, and exile from Venice for adultery before he arrived in Vienna, penniless and virtually unknown, in 1782. Within little more than a year, and despite his complete lack of experience as a librettist, he had talked himself into the top poetic job in the empire – the post of poet to the imperial theaters. (His later career included the establishment in London of England's first Italian bookshop and a number of years as a grocer in New Jersey. He ended his days, aged eighty-nine, as the first professor of Italian language and literature at Columbia College in New York.) A master of theatrical politics, he may well have been as influential as his (generally none too reliable) memoirs claimed in securing the Emperor's support for the project.

Little is known about the origins or development of Mozart's partnership with da Ponte, or about the composition of *Figaro*, but there are some grounds for believing the story that the bulk of the work was done in about six weeks towards the end of 1785. The run-up to the première in the Burgtheater on May 1, 1786, however, was beset with cabals and intrigues (some apparently involving Mozart's rival, Salieri), and the Irish tenor Michael Kelly, who created the roles of Don Basilio and Don Curzio in the new opera, later described Mozart as being 'touchy as gunpowder' during this period. His nervousness may have been aggravated by the fact that, as da Ponte stressed in his introduction to the libretto, *Figaro* was very much a new kind of entertainment and one which took the Italian *opera buffa* into uncharted social and musical territory. If so, he need not have worried. Despite the best efforts of the hired detractors who hissed from the gallery, the opera was generally well received on the first night, and on the second and third nights so many numbers had to be encored that the Emperor stepped in personally to limit repeats in future performances.

From the first *pianissimo* scurry of the overture to the unprecedented musical spans of the finales, the revolutionary nature of *Figaro* lies not in the supposedly seditious undertones of its plot but in the fabric of the music itself. Together with its rich social comedy and psychological acuity, the beauty of that music has ensured it a permanent and unrivaled place in the operatic repertoire.

But amid the success of *Figaro*, which was soon playing to appreciative audiences elsewhere in Germany, there were disturbing signs that neither Mozart's reputation nor his financial situation were secure. After his crowded schedule during Lent the previous year, he had given only one concert in the 1786 season and his academy concert on April 7 was to be his last in the official Burgtheater. More ominous still is the note he wrote to his publisher, Hoffmeister, at the end of November 1785, asking urgently for a loan. It is the first example of the begging letters that were to become all too frequent and depressing a part of Mozart's life during the second half of his decade in Vienna.

The Final Years

Few biographical stories have been overlaid by as many myths and half-truths as that of Mozart's last years. The romanticized version, re-created most notably in Peter Shaffer's imaginative but unhistorical *Amadeus*, became current soon after the composer's death, and its main features are well known: the childlike genius, unable to cope with the demands of everyday life, falls into poverty, despair and obscurity, dies under mysterious circumstances while writing a Requiem Mass commissioned by an anonymous stranger, and is buried in a pauper's grave, forgotten by a world incapable of recognizing his talents.

The reality is rather different. In fact, very little of this version of events survives closer scrutiny. That there was a marked discrepancy between Mozart's personality as a man and his personality as a composer is obvious enough to anyone who reads his letters, as is the streak of naivety, not to say childishness, that runs throughout them. Nannerl, writing after her brother's death (and admittedly with little first-hand knowledge of his final decade) claimed that 'except for his music he remained a *child*', and others' reminiscences, too, point to a limited ability to organize his own affairs. Beyond this, however, legend and truth diverge.

The pitiful begging letters Mozart wrote to his brother-mason Michael Puchberg confirm that he was deeply in debt for long periods during his last years. However, what we know of his actual earnings shows that the Mozarts were far from poverty stricken. The composer's income certainly fluctuated, but its average level was well above that of many of his fellow musicians and corresponded approximately to that of the highest non-noble tier of the civil service at the time. Nor was Mozart's standard of living that of a man in penury. The inventory of possessions taken immediately after his death includes fine furniture and an extensive wardrobe and, apart from the absence of disposable cash, paints a picture of very comfortable material circumstances. His last apartment, in the Rauhensteingasse, was less lavish than some he had lived in but it was hardly a garret, and even at the height of their financial difficulties the Mozarts, like most members of their class in the Vienna of the 1780s, employed their own domestic staff, including two live-in maids and a servant called Joseph (whom Mozart nicknamed 'Primus' to distinguish him from his more elevated namesake the Emperor Joseph II (Secundus)). Furthermore, Mozart's recorded income in his final year, 1791, was only marginally lower than that of Joseph Haydn, then making a handsome fortune from the first of what are regarded as his fantastically profitable concert seasons in London. In other words, Mozart's undoubtedly acute financial problems seem to have derived not from a low income but from cashflow difficulties and an expensive lifestyle. It is also worth remembering that before the advent of a modern banking system sizable loans between friends were a common feature of middle-class life, that Mozart lent money as well as borrowed it during his Vienna years, and that Constanze was in a position to lend out considerable sums herself within a few years of her husband's death.

Equally false is the belief that Mozart died in obscurity. There had certainly been a falling off in his *popularity*, both as pianist and as composer, in Vienna in the late 1780s, but even among the increasing number of people who found his later music 'difficult' there was seldom any doubt about the extraordinary nature of his gifts. At the time of his death he was by any standards a famous man, whose works were performed, studied and eulogized throughout Europe. The day after he died (according to his sister-in-law), 'crowds of people walked past his corpse and wept and wailed for him'; in

Prague, less than two weeks after his death, more than 4,000 people turned out for a memorial service in his honor; and numerous obituaries paid glowing tribute to his genius.

St Stephen's Cathedral, Vienna, the scene of Mozart's marriage in 1782 and his funeral in 1791

THE DEATH OF LEOPOLD

Mozart's output during the years 1786 to 1791 contains some of the greatest music of the classical or, for that matter, of any other period. Although there were, by the standards of his earlier Vienna years, long periods during which he wrote little or nothing in the way of major works, the half-decade after the first performance of *Figaro* saw a continuation of the creative flowering that began around the time of *Idomeneo* and continued until his death. To this period belong, among other things, the operas *Don Giovanni, Così fan tutte* and *Die Zauberflöte*, his four finest symphonies, three piano concertos, the divertimento for violin, viola and cello, four string quartets, the great string quintets in C major and G minor, the clarinet quintet and concerto and the unfinished Requiem, as well as a host of occasional works (including the dances he was required to produce under the terms of his contract as Kammermusicus (chamber musician) to the imperial court after December 1787) which fully confirm the truth of Leopold's dictum that 'what is slight can still be great'.

Yet the clouds that were already gathering on Mozart's financial horizon at the end of 1785 were not dispersed by the success of *Figaro*. As with all his operas, he received only a one-off fee for the work (in this case 450 florins) and future performances, however successful, brought him nothing more than reputation. In fact, if the income we can verify from surviving documents bears any relation to the total sums Mozart received, 1786 seems to have been the leanest of all his Vienna years.

The first Susanna: Mozart's friend and colleague, the English soprano Nancy Storace

It was no doubt with the state of his finances in mind that he approached his father in November with the proposal that Leopold should take care of little Karl and their newborn son Johann Thomas Leopold while he and Constanze traveled to England. Ever since his childhood successes in London, Mozart seems to have felt a particular affinity for England, and the desire to try his luck there again was almost certainly prompted by the various English friends he had in Vienna at this time, who included his pupil Thomas Attwood (later organist of St. Paul's and composer to the Chapel Royal), the theatrical composer Stephen Storace and his sister Nancy Storace, the first Susanna in *Figaro*. Presumably the plan had been for the Mozarts to accompany them and Michael Kelly on their way to England the following year, since Leopold gave the Storace-Attwood-Kelly party a guided tour of Salzburg when they broke their homeward journey there in February 1787. If so, this was the limit of Leopold's hospitality as far as the trip was concerned: he rejected 'very emphatically' his son's babysitting plan (though he was unaware that the new baby had died in the interim).

Instead, at the beginning of January 1787, Mozart and Constanze traveled (in considerable style) to Prague, where *Figaro* had been performed to huge acclaim in December. Whereas the opera was yesterday's news in Vienna (where, despite its initial success, it had been taken off after nine performances), in Prague it was still all the rage. 'Here', Mozart wrote to his friend the Baron von Jacquin on January 15, 'they talk about nothing but *Figaro*. Nothing is played, sung or whistled but *Figaro*. No opera is drawing like *Figaro*. Nothing, nothing but *Figaro*. Certainly a great honor for me!' The very evening of their arrival Mozart attended a ball at which many of the dances were arrangements of numbers from the opera. On the seventeenth it was given at the National Theater in Mozart's honor and a few days later he directed it there himself, conducting, as was his usual practice, from the keyboard. In between these two performances Mozart had given a public concert at the same theater, the program of which included a specially written symphony (K504, now known as the 'Prague') and an improvised set of variations on Figaro's showpiece aria 'Non più andrai'. When the Mozarts returned to Vienna in February their baggage included a commission from the impresario Bondini for an opera to be written for the next Prague season.

In April Mozart may or may not have given lessons to Beethoven, then a promising sixteen-year-old who had just arrived from Bonn to study with him; but despite romanticized versions there are no authenticated accounts of their meeting. Beethoven's stay was, in any case, a very brief one; his mother's fatal illness recalled him to Bonn after a few days and he did not return to Vienna until the year after Mozart's death.

A far more significant event in Mozart's life occurred the following month. At the beginning of April he had heard that his father was seriously ill in Salzburg and wrote him a letter that, with its philosophical poise and veiled masonic references, is often quoted as an example of Mozart's wisdom in the face of mortality. Under the circumstances, however, the abrupt transition from wishing Leopold well to assuring him of his own calm detachment at the prospect of death could also be read as more than a little insensitive:

Beethoven um 1786.

The young Ludwig van Beethoven, who may have met Mozart the year after this silhouette was made

I need hardly tell you how greatly I am longing to receive some reassuring news from yourself. And I still expect it; although I have now made a habit of being prepared in all affairs of life for the worst. As death, when we come to consider it closely, is the true goal of our existence, I have formed during the last few years such close relations with this best and truest friend of mankind, that his image is not only no longer terrifying to me, but is indeed very soothing and consoling! And I thank my God for graciously granting me the opportunity (you know what I mean) of learning that death is the key which unlocks the door to our true happiness. I never lie down at night without reflecting that – young as I am – I may not live to see another day. Yet no one of all my acquaintances could say that in company I am morose or disgruntled.

Leopold died on May 28, 1787 and was buried in Salzburg. Mozart, Nannerl and her husband settled on 1,000 gulden as Mozart's portion of the estate. Leopold's musical legacy to his son, however, was incalculably greater. As the lasting reputation of his *Violinschule* shows, Leopold was a formidable teacher, and his early contribution was unquestionably crucial in shaping the rounded musician Mozart became. For all his counting-house ways, contemporaries' reiterated praise for his sensitive paternal guidance is surely nearer the mark than the caricature sometimes presented by modern commentators of a money-grubbing exploiter of his children's talents. It is a tragedy that this fundamentally good-natured man, whose life had been lived vicariously through his child ever since the latter's extraordinary talents had revealed themselves, should in the end have come to feel himself spurned and neglected as Wolfgang inevitably grew away from him, leaving him a distant and increasingly embittered observer of the career he had launched so spectacularly on the world in those early years.

DON GIOVANNI

'You can imagine the state I am in!' Mozart wrote to his friend von Jacquin on hearing the news of his father's death, and there is no reason to doubt the genuineness of his grief. At the same time, he had little leisure to reflect on it. In addition to his teaching commitments, which included giving lessons to the eight-year-old Johann Nepomuk Hummel, later one of the foremost piano virtuosos of his time, he was busily engaged on his second collaboration with da Ponte – the *opera buffa Il dissoluto punito* or *Il Don Giovanni* K527. This was the work Bondini had commissioned during the Mozarts' visit to Prague earlier in the year and the première was scheduled to take place in that city on October 14 as part of the celebrations for a royal wedding. Even so, Mozart found time to write *Ein Musikalischer Spass* K522 – the 'musical joke' of the title being at the expense of second-rate composers and performers – and the almost soullessly perfect *Eine Kleine Nachtmusik* ('A little night-music') K525 before he and Constanze set off for Prague on October 1.

Don Giovanni seduces Zerlina in an 1841 production in Berlin

By this stage most of the music for the opera must have been completed, but there is reason to believe the traditional story that the overture – with its prefigurations of the climactic supper scene at which Don Giovanni is dragged down to hell by the ghost of the Commendatore he has murdered – was written in a single day only forty-eight hours before the first performance. In the event, the original schedule for the opera proved too tight to be practicable and the première was delayed until October 29, Mozart conducting instead a gala performance of *Figaro* for the royal wedding celebrations.

Despite the shortness of the rehearsal time, the often disorienting fusion of tragic and comic elements in the work and the ground-breaking complexity of some of its musical ideas, *Don Giovanni* was a resounding success. (Appropriately enough, given the libertine nature of the opera's eponymous hero, the audience on the first night probably included da Ponte's old friend Casanova.) According to the Prague press reports, there was a larger than average attendance, Mozart himself was given three rousing cheers when he entered the orchestra pit and again when he left it and both singers and orchestra excelled themselves in their desire to do credit to the composer. Mozart himself wrote to von Jacquin that the opera had been received with 'the greatest applause'. He directed three performances himself and a fourth was given for his benefit.

After spending some time with their friends the Duscheks in the Bertramka Villa outside Prague, the Mozarts returned to Vienna in mid-November. Shortly afterwards Mozart finally received the tangible token of imperial favor he had been hoping for ever since his arrival in the city in 1781. On December 7 Joseph II appointed him court Kammermusicus (chamber musician). The post was not an onerous one – Mozart's duties amounted to little more than the composition of dances for court balls – but neither did it carry a large salary. The previous incumbent, the great operatic composer

*The masked figures
from the finale to Act I
of* Don Giovanni:
*1987 Salzburg Festival
costume designs*

*The musicians from
the finale to Act II
of* Don Giovanni:
*1987 Salzburg Festival
costume designs*

Christoph Willibald von Gluck, who had just died, had received 2,000 gulden per annum; Mozart received only 800. It was hardly the eminent Kapellmeister post Leopold had urged his son to aim for, but it was at least a court appointment and provided him with a regular source of income for the first time in nearly six years. Besides, Mozart was not shy about calling himself, or letting himself be called, Kapellmeister regardless of his official title. It seems likely that the appointment was made to deter Mozart from seeking employment elsewhere. There was, after all, every reason to think he might do so. His plans to visit England had found their way into the newspapers, and the very month his contract as Kammermusicus was drawn up Haydn had fulminated to the chief of commissariat in Prague against the short-sightedness of those 'great ones' who failed to give 'this *unique* Mozart' a permanent position. Indeed, at the beginning of 1788, after Mozart's recent successes in Prague, the contrast between his fortunes inside and outside Vienna was only too obvious. On May 7 *Don Giovanni* was given its Vienna première, and although it was not the flop of popular legend, it certainly met with nothing like the rapture that had greeted it in Prague, and after 1788 *Don Giovanni* was never performed again in Vienna in Mozart's lifetime.

In June he had to withdraw his string quintets from publication, having failed to find enough subscribers for them, perhaps because so many of the nobility were away fighting alongside Russia in the Turkish war, and the same month saw the first (or the first that has survived) of the increasingly desperate begging letters he wrote to his friend and fellow mason, the businessman Michael Puchberg. (Over the next three years Puchberg was to lend Mozart the substantial sum of more than 1,400 gulden, some of which the composer may have repaid by the time of his death.) In June, too, the Mozarts lost their fourth child, Theresia, who had been born the previous December. They also made another of their frequent moves, this time back to the suburbs and cheaper accommodation, where Mozart found it easier to work, despite the 'black thoughts' which he told Puchberg often oppressed him and which he banished only with a tremendous effort of will.

Astonishingly, it was under these circumstances that Mozart wrote his three last symphonies, No. 39 in E♭ (K543), No. 40 in G minor (K550) and No. 41 in C (the 'Jupiter', K551), entering them into his thematic catalog over a period of just six weeks between June 26 and August 10. These strongly contrasting works mark the summit of Mozart's achievement as a symphonist and are among the greatest in the symphonic canon. The last movement of the 'Jupiter', with its towering counterpoint, is perhaps Mozart's finest piece of symphonic writing. The occasion of the symphonies' composition is unknown, and Romantic commentators tended to see them as a spontaneous uprush of inspiration or as a conscious symphonic swansong. Given Mozart's customary working practice, however, it is extremely unlikely that they were written without a specific performance in mind, though it is uncertain whether such performance actually took place.

The Danish actor and musician, Joachim Preisler, has left a vivid picture of the Mozart household at this time. On August 24, 1788 he and three colleagues visited the composer's flat in the Währingerstrasse, where, he recalls:

I had the happiest hour of music that has ever fallen to my lot. This small man and great master twice extemporized *on a* pedal pianoforte, *so wonderfully! so wonderfully! that I quite lost myself. He intertwined the most difficult passages with the most lovely* themes. – *His wife cut quill-pens for the copyist, a pupil composed, a little boy {Karl} aged four walked about in the garden and sang recitatives – in short, everything that surrounded this splended man was* musical! *I thought with pleasure of his* Entführung aus dem Serail, *which I had heard at Hamburg in 1787, and which I know almost by heart, but he called this operetta a trifle. . . .*

It is perhaps indicative of the musical territory into which Mozart was now moving that he should have dismissed so lightly what was at the time his most popular opera. There had always been commentators who found his music 'difficult', both to play and to understand, but from about this time such criticisms become more frequent, partly, no doubt, because the technical demands imposed by his late style resulted in inadequate performances. Also frequently commented on is Mozart's textural complexity, what one contemporary critic called his 'overloading of instrumental detail'; and even professional musicians seem to have found it hard to assimilate the sheer profusion of his ideas. Haydn was speaking for posterity when he wrote in 1787 of 'Mozart's incomparable works, *so profound* and so full of *musical intelligence*', but the *Magazin der Musik* was speaking for an increasing number of his contemporaries when in 1788, comparing him to a prominent rival, one of its correspondents reported from Vienna: 'Kozeluch's works hold their ground, and are always acceptable, but Mozart's are not by any means so popular.'

'FATE IS SO MUCH AGAINST ME . . .'

It has been calculated that between 1784 and 1788 Mozart was producing new works at an average rate of one every eighteen days. More astonishing still is the fact that of more than 100 works completed during this period, some four-fifths can be counted among his masterpieces. In 1789 and 1790, however, Mozart's productivity declined, at least as far as major works are concerned. The survival of many more sketches from Mozart's last three years may indicate that he was finding composition a slower process than heretofore. Certainly, they show the limits of the traditional view that he composed every work completely in his mind, regardless of its scale or complexity, before putting pen to paper. (In fact, his normal practice with large-scale compositions seems to have been to plan a work mentally from beginning to end, then to write it out in *particella* form, i.e. with top and bottom parts and any others he needed to jog his memory, and finally to fill in the remaining parts, making separate sketches for passages of particular complexity; recent studies have shown that some works would be left in *particella* form for long periods before being completed.)

The longer intervals between major works during this time may also reflect the cumulatively demoralizing effect of Mozart's financial difficulties. There are another four letters to Puchberg asking for loans in 1789 and a further nine in 1790. In one particularly distressing example, from July 12, 1789, Mozart reports that both he and his wife have been ill, as a result of which he has been unable to work, and that the subscription list he has been circulating for a projected concert has returned with only one name on it, that of his long-standing patron van Swieten. The striking contrast with the 176 names on his 1784 subscription list is an indication of how far Mozart's popularity, as well perhaps as the material circumstances of the Viennese nobility, hard hit as they were by Joseph's reforms and the economic effects of his Turkish war, had declined over the last five years. 'Fate is so much against me,' he wrote in the same letter, *'though only in Vienna*, that even when I want to, I cannot make any money.'

The qualification is significant. Although in Vienna Mozart was having to rely for income on such journeyman work as arranging pieces by Handel, elsewhere he was still in demand as a performer and composer. In April and May 1789 he accompanied his friend and fellow mason, Countess Thun's son-in-law Prince Karl Lichnowsky, to Berlin (the Prince paid for the journey and Mozart borrowed money for his incidental expenses). They called *en route* at Prague, where Mozart renewed his acquaintance with Bondini's successor, the impresario Guardasoni, and apparently came close to finalizing an opera contract with him. He then continued to Dresden, where he gave a private concert, the program of which included the Divertimento for String Trio (K563) he had written for Puchberg. He also played before the Electress at court (his penultimate piano concerto (K537), now known as the 'Coronation', because he performed it again at Leopold II's coronation in Frankfurt the following year), took part in a musical duel with the organist Hässler, and was sketched, looking decidedly unhealthy, by Doris Stock – the most talented artist to portray him during his lifetime. In addition, he shuttled between Potsdam and Leipzig, where he played the organ in the church at which J. S. Bach had been Kantor for so many years and gave a marathon but poorly attended concert with his Prague friend Josepha Duschek, before arriving in Berlin itself. Here he performed before Frederick William II of Prussia, a keen amateur cellist, and

Above:
Silhouette of Mozart's brother-in-law, Joseph Lange, in 1785

Right:
Mozart at the piano, 1789/90: the famous unfinished portrait by Joseph Lange

was probably commissioned to compose six string quartets for the king and six piano sonatas for his daughter. (His last three quartets may be the result of this commission.) It is clear from his regular letters to Constanze that Mozart missed his wife dreadfully during the two-month trip, though he seems also to have underplayed to her the amount of money he made from it.

On June 4, 1789 the couple were reunited in Vienna, only to be separated again in August when Constanze went to Baden, a fashionable (and expensive) spa near the city, to convalesce from what seems to have been her serious illness of the previous month. Mozart visited her there when he could, while also working on new material for a revival of *Figaro* which took place at the Burgtheater on the twenty-ninth. On November 16 Constanze gave birth to their fifth child, a girl, who died the same day.

Poster advertising the première of Così fan tutte *at the Burgtheater in Vienna, 26 January 1790*

During this period Mozart was also working on a new opera, *Così fan tutte* or *La scuola degli amanti* (*All women behave that way* or *The school for lovers*) K588, the last on which he was to collaborate with da Ponte; and a few days before rehearsals began at the end of December, the wistful Clarinet Quintet K581, composed like a later concerto for his clarinettist friend Anton Stadler, was performed at a concert given by the Tonkünstler-Sozietät (a musicians' mutual support association which Mozart was technically ineligible to join, having mislaid his birth certificate).

The Emperor Leopold II in his coronation robes

The circumstances under which *Così* was commissioned are unclear, but the première took place at the Burgtheater on January 26, 1790 and was well received. However, the initial run of performances was interrupted by the death in February of the Emperor Joseph II, and although the opera was revived in the summer, it thereafter appeared only sporadically in the repertoire until the twentieth century. The work contains some of Mozart's most beautiful operatic writing, but the plot, which turns on the systematic and cynical deception of two sisters by their lovers, was felt by many high-minded nineteenth-century Romantics (including Beethoven) to be unworthy of the music, to the extent that entirely new texts were sometimes written for it.

Mozart saw the accession of the new Emperor, Joseph's brother Leopold II, as an opportunity to be grasped. In May he petitioned the royal family, unsuccessfully, for the post of second Kapellmeister, then in September he and Franz Hofer, the husband of Constanze's sister Josepha, set off for Frankfurt to make what musical capital they could out of Leopold's coronation, which took place in the cathedral on October 9. Unlike Kapellmeister Salieri (who was by no means the irredeemable mediocrity of legend), Mozart had no official role in the celebrations, and the public concert he gave on October 15 (the one that provided the 'Coronation' concerto with its nickname) was not well enough attended for him to go ahead with a projected second one two days later. On his way home, he played at the electoral palace in Mainz, attended the first Mannheim performance of *Figaro* (the first time he had heard it sung in German), and performed before the King of Naples at Munich. In mid-November he rejoined Constanze, now back in Vienna after another rest cure at Baden, in the new lodgings in the Rauhensteingasse into which she and Karl had moved while he was away. It was the last apartment Mozart would occupy.

THE LAST YEAR

As Mozart's final year dawned, his prospects were clearly improving. Towards the end of 1790 he had received two offers from London impresarios, most recently from Johann Peter Salomon, whom he had met at a farewell party for Joseph Haydn on December 14. Haydn was about to leave for the first of the highly profitable London concert series which Salomon had arranged, and it seems that Salomon had Mozart penciled in for the following winter. One account has Mozart telling the departing Haydn that this was the last time the two men would see each other alive, but if there

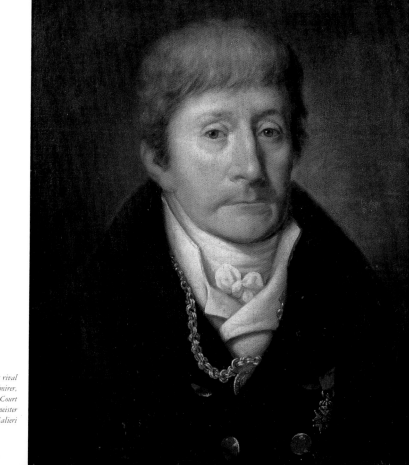

*Mozart's rival
and admirer,
the Vienna Court
Kapellmeister
Antonio Salieri*

is any truth in the story it is more likely to derive from Haydn's relatively advanced age than from any premonitions of an early grave. Be that as it may, the following winter Mozart was already dead.

In March, at the Jahnscher Saal, a concert room just across the road from his apartment, Mozart was well received at what proved to be his last public concert appearance. He played the Piano Concerto in B♭ K595 – his last, and a work in which, as so often in Mozart's final years, the dividing line between laughter and tears is particularly finely drawn. Later in the spring he petitioned for, and was granted, the unpaid post of assistant to Leopold Hofmann, the ailing Kapellmeister of St. Stephen's Cathedral, on the understanding that he would graduate to the prestigious (and highly paid) post of Kapellmeister on Hofmann's imminently expected death. (As it happened, Hofmann outlived him by fifteen months.)

Furthermore, Mozart was snowed under with commissions during the year, including three for lucrative major works. In the spring the actor-manager Emanuel Schikaneder, whom Mozart had known since his Salzburg days, signed him up to write an opera, *Die Zauberflöte (The magic flute),* for his theater in the Viennese suburbs. Then, in July, the impresario Guardasoni commissioned him to compose – at very short notice – a 'festival opera', *La clemenza di Tito (The clemency of Titus)* K621, to be given in Prague in September as part of the official celebrations for the Emperor's coronation as King of Bohemia.

The third major commission, which Mozart seems to have received shortly before Guardasoni contacted him about *La clemenza di Tito*, has done more than anything else to fuel the myths surrounding his last months. According to Constanze, who told the story to Mozart's first biographer, her husband was approached by an anonymous messenger and asked to quote his price for composing a requiem (a mass for the dead).

The intermediary declined to name the person for whom he was acting and urged Mozart not to try to discover his identity. We now know that the patron was one Count Walsegg-Stuppach, an eccentric and rather pathetic character who lived in a remote Austrian castle (as well as owning the house in Vienna in which Michael Puchberg lived) and liked to think he succeeded in passing off other composers' work as his own. The Requiem was intended to commemorate his recently deceased wife.

Set design from a 1799 performance of La clemenza di Tito *at the Frankfurt Nationaltheater*

Given these contracts, it is perhaps not surprising that the tone of Mozart's three surviving letters to Puchberg during the first half of 1791 is now calmly business-like, that the loans he requested were small and short-term, and that in July he could promise to send him the enormous sum of 2,000 gulden within a few days. He seems also to have been able to afford to place Karl at an expensive private school and to pay for two further rest cures for Constanze at Baden (during the first of which, in the summer, he wrote the short but breathtakingly lovely motet *Ave verum corpus* K618 for the choirmaster at the local parish church). As if to underline the upturn in their fortunes, the Mozarts' last child, Franz Xaver Wolfgang, who was born on July 26, became only the second of their six offspring to survive. (He later became a musician but, despite Constanze's attempts to promote him as a child prodigy, he never emerged from his father's shadow. He died in 1844.)

It is also not surprising that Mozart was beginning to show signs of exhaustion from overwork. At the end of August he and Constanze left Vienna for Prague, Mozart continuing his work on *Tito* during the three-day coach journey; the secco recitatives he subcontracted to his pupil Franz Xaver Süssmayr, who also traveled with the couple. In contrast to the coronation in Frankfurt the previous year, Mozart's music featured throughout the Prague celebrations: within four days of arriving, for example, the Emperor attended a performance of *Don Giovanni* at the National Theater – one eye-witness spotted Mozart among the audience ('a little man in a green coat, whose eye reveals what his modest condition hides') – and a number of Mozart's sacred works were also performed during the festivities.

The Queen of the Night from an 1818 Munich production of Die Zauberflöte

Mozart conducted the première of *Tito* in the National Theater on coronation day itself, September 6, having only completed the opera the day before. This grand first performance seems not to have been an unqualified success – certainly, the Empress was very rude about it – and the work still enjoys a more mixed critical reputation than any of Mozart's other mature operas, perhaps because his lyrically concise late style sits uneasily with the archaic flavor of its *opera seria* conventions. That said, after a generally poorly attended run, at its last performance on September 30 (by which time the Mozarts were back in Vienna) it was greeted with rapturous applause and there were those in the years following Mozart's death who regarded it as his greatest opera.

The very same evening that *Tito* closed in Prague, Mozart conducted the first performance of *Die Zauberflöte* in Vienna. The new opera was a very different creation from *Tito*. With its spoken dialogue and its curious mixture of masonic, magical and comic elements, it belongs in the tradition of the German *Singspiel*. The diversity of its music is kaleidoscopic, ranging from the catchy folk-like melodies of Papageno the birdcatcher to the sublime duet 'Bei Männern, welche Liebe fühlen' and the austere chorale of the armored men in the final act. The circumstances for which it was written were very different too. *Tito* was performed as the musical centerpiece to an occasion of imperial pomp and grandeur. *Die Zauberflöte* was designed for a suburban theater – the Theater auf der Wieden, also known as the Freyhaustheater, from the name of the warren of

Karl Friedrich Schinkel's monumental stage set for the 1816 Berlin performance of Die Zauberflöte

apartments and business premises in which it stood – and a predominantly bourgeois audience. Schikaneder, an unashamed populist who had acquired the theater a couple of years earlier, wrote the libretto and also took the part of Papageno, Mozart's sister-in-law Josepha Hofer playing the Queen of the Night.

After a shaky start, the opera became a huge box-office success and was soon drawing such notables as Count Zinzendorf out to the suburbs to see it. Mozart reported to Constanze, who was back in Baden with Süssmayr, that he had ferried Salieri and his mistress to one of the twenty or so performances that took place in October and that his old rival was quite carried away by it, shouting 'bravo!' or 'bello!' after almost every number. Mercurial as ever, one evening Mozart stormed out of a box when its occupant refused to understand the serious messages of the opera, only to sneak backstage later in the same performance and play the glockenspiel out of synch with Papageno's mimed actions on the stage – a practical joke

Papageno: costume design from an 1816 performance of Die Zauberflöte *in Berlin*

which amused the audience more than it did the discomfited Schikaneder. While *Die Zauberflöte* was playing to packed houses, and looking set to exceed *Die Entführung* in popularity, Mozart completed his last instrumental work, the famously autumnal clarinet concerto K622, and sent it off to Prague where his friend Stadler, who had stayed behind after playing in the orchestra for *Tito*, gave it its first performance on October 16.

All in all, there is little in Mozart's first-hand accounts of his life at this time to endorse the popular view that he was suffering from depression, let alone the delusion

How nineteenth-century Romantics saw it:
Mozart rehearses the Requiem on his deathbed

that he was writing the Requiem, on which he had now resumed work, for his own funeral. On the contrary, his letters to Constanze at Baden are full of high spirits, uninhibited affection and rather heavy-handed jokes at the expense of Süssmayr. (Actually, there is very little in the whole of Mozart's correspondence to suggest a depressive personality; with the exception of some written at the very nadir of his financial fortunes, the passages most often quoted in this context almost all belong to periods of separation from Constanze and refer specifically to his longing to be with her again.) Work on the Requiem itself seems to have progressed rapidly once his other compositional commitments were out of the way, and while he was undoubtedly inundated with work, it was nothing his apparently undiminished powers of concentration had not proved able to cope with in the past. None the less, the story of dark delusions in his final weeks does have to be taken seriously, not least because it appears in the early biographies of the composer which were written under Constanze's own guidance, and according to which she had to take the score of the Requiem away from him and seek to divert his attention to more cheerful matters in an attempt to preserve his deteriorating mental balance.

Whatever the truth, on November 18, Mozart became suddenly and seriously ill after attending a performance of his last completed work, the masonic cantata K623, at a meeting of his lodge. It seems likely that this collapse was related to other bouts of illness he had suffered at intervals throughout his adult life and which seem often to have coincided with periods of intense overwork (most recently in Prague during the frenetic final stages of composing *La clemenza di Tito*). Retrospective modern diagnosis – always a dangerous science – favors the theory that it was a form of recurrent rheumatic fever, perhaps first contracted in childhood. Mozart may have believed at one stage that he had been poisoned, but there is not the slightest evidence that he was, or for that matter that Salieri – despite his self-accusatory deathbed ravings more than thirty years later – was in any way connected with his death.

On November 20, Mozart took to his bed and a week later his two personal doctors met to discuss his condition. On December 4, he appeared stronger and may have been able to direct a small rehearsal of the still unfinished Requiem at his bedside. Later the same day, however, his condition deteriorated sharply, though according to his youngest sister-in-law Sophie, who many years later wrote a deeply moving account of his last hours, he was still lucid enough to give Süssmayr instructions on how he wanted the Requiem to be completed in the event of his death. Shortly afterwards, apparently after being treated with cold poultices, he fell into a coma from which he never recovered. He died at five minutes to one in the morning of December 5, 1791, at the age of thirty-five.

The house in the Rauhenstrasse where Mozart died on 5 December 1791

CODA

Entry for Mozart in the Register of Deaths of St Stephen's, Vienna, 6 December 1791

Mozart's body was buried two days later in the suburban cemetery of St. Marx. The pauper's grave is a myth, as are the rain and snowstorms that are said to have accompanied his body to its last resting place. He was given a third-class funeral, conducted in accordance with the reformed rules on burial practice introduced by Joseph II, and the weather was unseasonally mild. There is no reliable evidence as to who if anyone was present at the graveside, but van Swieten, Süssmayr and Salieri (whose undoubted intrigues against Mozart over the preceding decade were leavened, as we have seen, with deep professional respect), may well have been among the mourners. The site of the grave can no longer be determined with certainty.

Van Swieten, despite having other things on his mind (the very day of Mozart's death he was dismissed from his post in the new Emperor's clear-out of his brother's personnel), tendered valuable help to the composer's widow and children, as did other well-wishers. Initially hysterical at her husband's death, Constanze succeeded in persuading the court to grant her a pension, even though Mozart's period of service as Kammermusicus had officially been too short for her to qualify. She supervised Süssmayr's completion of the Requiem and, in order to ensure payment of the agreed fee, disguised the fact that it was not all her husband's work. Count Walsegg conducted it at Wiener Neustadt in December 1793, though it had received its first performance at van Swieten's instigation in Vienna earlier the same year.

Constanze devoted a large part of the ensuing years to promoting performances of Mozart's works and arranging their publication. In 1809 she married the Danish diplomat Georg Nikolaus Nissen, with whom she lived in Copenhagen until 1820 when they moved to Salzburg. There Nissen spent much of his remaining six years of life working with his wife on a substantial biography of her first husband. After his death, her sister Sophie (whose own husband died the same year) went to live with Constanze in the town where Mozart had been born and which he detested so vehemently. Nannerl had also moved back to Salzburg after her husband's death in 1801 (she died there in 1829, aged 78), but the two sisters-in-law seem not to have sought one another out. Both became objects of pilgrimage by lovers of Mozart's music and furnished enquirers with numerous personal reminiscences of the composer in their later years.

Constanze died in 1842 at the age of 80. By the time of her death, and owing in no small measure to her own unstinting efforts, her first husband's place in the musical pantheon was assured. Through all the musical revolutions of the intervening years, it has remained so unassailably to this day.

The memorial marking the putative site of Mozart's grave in the St Marx cemetery, Vienna

mozart

the complete works

Mozart did not number his works. They were chronologically catalogued by Ludwig von Köchel in 1862 and each was given a 'Köchel number'. Further research has slightly altered the order and, where relevant, the latest revisions follow the original K number. Some of the works ascribed to Mozart are now thought to be of doubtful authorship and they are not included in the following list. Dates are given where known.

K1*a*	Andante, C major (1761)
K1*b*	Allegro, C major (1761)
K1*c*	Allegro, F major (1761)
K1*d*	Minuet, F major (1761)
K1/1*e*	Minuet, G major (1761–2)
K1*f*	Minuet, C major (1761–2)
KA1/297*a*	Miserere (1778)
K2	Minuet, F major (1762)
KA2/73A	Misero tu non sei (1770)
K3	Allegro, B♭ major (1762)
KA3/315*b*	[Scena] (1778)
K4	Minuet, F major (1762)
K5	Minuet, F major (1762)
K5*a*	Allegro, C major (1763)
K5*b*	Andante, B♭ major (1763)
KA5/571*a*	Caro mio Druck und Schluck (1789)
K6	Violin and piano sonata, C major (1762–4)

March (1767)	K41*c*
Minuet (1767)	K41*d*
Fugue (1767)	K41*e*
Fugue a 4 (1767)	K41*f*
Nachtmusik (1767)	K41*g*
Cantata, Grabmusik (1767)	K42/35*a*
Symphony No. 6, F major (1767)	K43
Symphony No. 7, D major (1767)	K45
Violin sonata, C major (1768)	K46*d*
Violin sonata, F major (1768)	K46*e*
Veni, Sancte Spiritus, C major (1768)	K47
Trumpet concerto (1768)	K47*c*
Symphony No. 8, D major (1768)	K48
Missa brevis, G major (1768)	K49/47*d*
Bastien und Bastienne (1768)	K50 /46*b*
La finta semplice (1769)	K51/46*a*
An die Freude: Freude, Königin der Weisen, F major (1768)	K53/47*e*
Variation, F major (1788)	K54/547*b*
Minuet, C major (1770)	K61*g,ii*
March, D major (1769)	K62
Cassation, G major (1769)	K63
Missa brevis, D minor (1769)	K65/61*a*
7 minuets (1769)	K65*a*/61*b*
Missa, 'Domenicus', C major (1769)	K66

K67/41*b*	Church sonata No. 1, E♭ major (1772)
K68/41*i*	Church sonata No. 2, B♭ major (1772)
K69/41*k*	Church sonata No. 3, D major (1772)
K70/61*c*	A Berenice . . . Sol nascente (1766)
K71	Ah più tremar non voglio (c. 1770)
K72/74*f*	Inter natos mulierum, G major (1771)
K72*a*	Allegro, G major (1770)
K73	Symphony No. 9, C major (1772)
K74	Symphony No. 10, G major (1770)
K74*b*	Non curo l'affetto (1771)
K75	Symphony No. 42, F major (1771)
K76/42*a*	Symphony No. 43, F major (1767)
K77/73*e*	Misero me . . . Misero pargoletto (1770)
K78/73*b*	Per pietà, bell'idol mio (1766)
KA78/620*b*	[Contrapuntal study], B minor (1791)
K79/73*d*	O temerario Arbace . . .
	Per quel paterno amplesso (1766)
K80/73*f*	String quartet No. 1, G major (1770)
K81/73*l*	Symphony No. 44, D major (1770)
K82/73*o*	Se ardire, e speranza (1770)
K83/73*p*	Se tutti i mali miei (1770)
K84/73*q*	Symphony No. 11, D major (1770)
K85/73*s*	Miserere, A minor (1770)
K86/73*v*	Quaerite primum regnum Dei, D minor (1770)

K109/74*e*	Litany, B♭ major (1771)
KA109*b*/15*a-ss*	London Sketchbook (1765)
KA109*d*/73*x*	14 Canonic studies (1772)
KA109*g*/537*d*	Arrangement of C. P. E. Bach's, Ich folge dir (1788)
K110/75*b*	Symphony No. 12, G major (1771)
K111	Ascanio in Alba, festa teatrale (1771)
K112	Symphony No. 13, F major (1771)
K113	Divertimento, E♭ major (1771)
K114	Symphony No. 14, A major (1771)
K117/66*a*	Benedictus sit Deus, C major (1768)
K118/74*c*	La Betulia liberata (1771)
K119/382*b*	Der Liebe himmlisches Gefühl (1782)
K120/111*a*	Symphony No. 48, D major (1771)
K121/207*a*	Symphony No. 51, D major (1775)
K122/73*t*	Minuet, E♭ major (1770)
K123/73*g*	Contredanse, B♭ major (1770)
K124	Symphony No. 15, G major (1772)
K125	Litany, B♭ major (1772)
K126	Il sogno di Scipione (1772)
K127	Regina coeli, B♭ major (1772)
K128	Symphony No. 16, C major (1772)
K129	Symphony No. 17, G major (1772)
K130	Symphony No. 18, F major (1772)
K131	Divertimento, D major (1772)

Symphony No. 19, E♭ major (1772)	K132
Symphony No. 20, D major (1772)	K133
Symphony No. 21, A major (1772)	K134
Lucio Silla (1772)	K135
Piano sonata, F major (1788)	KA135/547*a*
String divertimento, D major (1772)	K136/125*a*
String divertimento, B♭ major (1772)	K137/125*b*
String divertimento, F major (1772)	K138/125*c*
Missa solemnis, 'Waisenhausmesse', C minor (1768)	K139/47*a*
Te Deum, C major (1769)	K141/66*b*
Ergo interest . . . Quaere superna, G major (1773)	K143/73*a*
Church sonata No.4, D major (1774)	K144/124*a*
Church sonata No.5, F major (1774)	K145/124*b*
Kommet her, ihr frechen Sünder, B♭ major (1779)	K146/317*b*
Wie unglücklich bin ich nit, F major (?1775–6)	K147/125*g*
Lobegesang auf die feierliche Johannisloge, D major (?1775–6)	K148/125*h*
Die grossmütige Gelassenheit (?1772)	K149/125*d*
Geheime Liebe:Was ich in Gedanken küsse (?1772)	K150/125*e*
Die Zufriedenheit im niedrigen Stande (?1772)	K151/125*f*
Fugue, E♭ major (1783)	K153/375*f*
Fugue, G minor (1782)	K154/385*k*
String quartet No. 2, D major (1772)	K155/134*a*
String quartet No. 3, G major (1772)	K156/134*b*

K157	String quartet No. 4, C major (1772–3)
K158	String quartet No. 5, F major (1772–3)
K159	String quartet No. 6, B♭ major (1773)
K160/159a	String quartet No 7, E♭ major (1773)
K161,K163/141a	Symphony No. 50, D major (1773–4)
K162	Symphony No. 22, C major (1773)
K164/130a	6 minuets (1772)
K165/158a	Exsultate, jubilate, F major (1773)
K166/159d	Divertimento, E♭ major (1773)
K167	Missa, 'In honorem Ssmae Trinitatis', C major (1773)
K168	String quartet No. 8, F major (1773)
K168a	Minuet, F major (1775)
K169	String quartet No. 9, A major (1773)
K170	String quartet No. 10, C major (1773)
K171	String quartet No, 11, E♭ major (1773)
KA171/285b	Flute quartet, C major (1781–2)
K172	String quartet No. 12, B♭ major (1773)
K173	String quartet No. 13, D minor (1773)
K174	String quintet No. 1, B♭ major (1773)
K175	Piano concerto No. 5, D major (1773)
K176	16 minuets (1773)
K178/417e	Ah, spiegarti, oh Dio (1783)
K179/189a	12 variations in C major (1774)
K180/173c	6 variations in G major (1773)

Symphony No.23, D major (1773)	K181/162*b*
Symphony No. 24, B♭ major (1773)	K182/173*dA*
Symphony No. 25, G minor (1773)	K183/173*dB*
Symphony No. 26, E♭ major (1773)	K184/161*a*
Serenade, Finalmusik, D major (1773)	K185/167*a*
Divertimento, B♭ major (1773)	K186/159*b*
Divertimento, C major (1773)	K188/240*b*
March, D major (1773)	K189/167*b*
Concertone, C major (1774)	K190/186*E*
Bassoon concerto, B♭ major (1774)	K191/186*e*
Canon, C major	KA191/562*c*
Missa brevis, F major (1774)	K192/186*f*
Dixit Dominus & Magnificat, C major (1774)	K193/186*g*
Missa brevis, D major (1774)	K194/186*h*
Litany, D major (1774)	K195/186*d*
La finta giardiniera (1775)	K196
Sub tuum praesidium, F major (1774)	K198/C3.08
Symphony No. 27, G major (1773)	K199/161*b*
Piano sonata, G major (1766)	KA199/33*d*
Symphony No. 28, C major (1774)	K200/189*k*
Piano sonata, B♭ major (1766)	KA200/33*e*
Symphony No. 29, A major (1774)	K201/186*a*
Piano sonata, C major (1766)	KA201/33*f*
Symphony No. 30, D major (1774)	K202/186*b*

KA202/33g	Piano sonata, F major (1766)
K203/189b	Serenade, D major (1774)
K204/213a	Serenade, D major (1775)
K205/167A	Divertimento, D major (1773)
K206	March, D major (1780)
KA206/21a	Variation, C major (1765)
K207	Violin concerto, B♭ major (1775)
KA207/C27.06	For Ascanio in Alba (1771)
K208	Il Rè pastore (1775)
K209	Si mostra la sorte (1775)
K210	Con ossequio, con rispetto (1775)
K211	Violin concerto, D major (1775)
K212	Church sonata No. 6, B♭ major (1775)
K213	Divertimento, F major (1775)
K214	March, C major (1775)
KA214/45b	Symphony No.55, B♭ major (1768)
K215/213b	March, D major (1775)
KA215/66c	Symphony, D major (1769)
K216	Violin concerto, G major (1775)
KA216/C11.03	Symphony, B♭ major (1770–1)
K217	Voi avete un cor fedele (1775)
KA217/66d	Symphony, B♭ major (1769)
K218	Violin concerto, D major (1775)
KA218/66e	Symphony, B♭ major (1769)

Violin concerto, A major (1775)	K219
Missa brevis, 'Spatzenmesse', G major, (1775–6)	K220/196*b*
Symphony, A minor? (1765)	K A220/16*a*
Symphony 'Alle Lambacher', G major (1768)	K A221/45*a*
Misericordias Domini, D minor (1775)	K222/205*a*
Symphony, C major (1765)	K A222/19*b*
Symphony, F major (1765)	K A223/19*a*
Church sonata No. 7, F major (1780)	K224/241*a*
Church sonata No. 8, A major (1780)	K225/241*b*
Ach, zu kurz ist unsers Lebens Lauf (1787)	K228/515*b*
Sie ist dahin, C minor (1782)	K229/382*a*
5 divertimentos, B♭ major (1783)	K A229/439*b*
Selig, selig alle, C minor (1782)	K230/382*b*
Leck mich im Arsch, B♭ major (1782)	K231/382*c*
Lieber Freistädtler, lieber Gaulimauli, G major (1787)	K232/509*a*
Leck mir den Arsch, B♭ major (1782)	K233/382*d*
Bei der Hitz' im Sommer ess ich, G major (1782)	K234/382*e*
Andantino, E♭ major	K236/588*b*
March, D major (1774)	K237/189*c*
Piano concerto No. 6, B♭ major (1776)	K238
Serenata notturna, D major (1776)	K239
Divertimento, B♭ major (1776)	K240
Church sonata No. 9, G major (1776)	K241
3 pianos concerto No. 7, F major (1776)	K242

K243	Litany, E♭ major (1776)
K244	Church sonata, No. 10, F major (1776)
K245	Church sonata No. 11, D major (1776)
KA245/621*a*	Io ti lascio, B major (1791)
K246	Piano concerto, No. 8, C major (1776)
K247	Divertimento, F major (1776)
K248	March, F major (1776)
K249	March, D major (1776)
K250/248*b*	Serenade 'Haffner', D major (1776)
K251/251	Divertimento, D major (1776)
K252/240*a*	Divertimento, E♭ major (1776)
K253	Divertimento, F major (1776)
K254	Divertimento (piano trio), B♭ major (1776)
K255	Ombra felice . . . Io ti lascio (1776)
K256	Clarice cara mia sposa (1776)
K257	Missa, 'Credo', C major (1776)
K258	Missa brevis, 'Spaur', C major (1776)
K259	Missa brevis, 'Organ solo', C major (1776)
K260/248*a*	Venite populi, D major (1776)
K261	Adagio, E major (1776)
K262/246*a*	Missa [longa], C major (1775)
K263	Church sonata No. 12, C major (1776)
K264/315*d*	9 variations, C major (1778)
K265/300*e*	12 variations, C major (1781–2)

Sonata (trio), B♭ major (1777)	K266/271*f*
4 Contredanses (1777)	K267/271*c*
Rondo, B♭ major (1776)	K269/261*a*
2 Contredanses for Count Czernin (1777)	K269*b*
Divertimento, B♭ major (1777)	K270
Piano concerto No. 9, E♭ major (1777)	K271
Oboe concerto, C major (1777)	K271*k*
Ah, lo previdi . . . Ah, t'invola agl'occhi miei (1777)	K272
Sancta Maria, mater Dei, F major (1777)	K273
Church sonata No. 13, G major (1777)	K274/271*d*
Missa brevis, B♭ major (1777)	K275/272*b*
Regina coeli, C major (1779)	K276/321*b*
Alma Dei creatoris, F major (1777)	K277/272*a*
Church sonata No. 14, C major (1777)	K278/271*e*
Piano sonata, C major (1775)	K279/189*d*
Piano sonata, F major (1775)	K280/189*e*
Piano sonata, B♭ major (1775)	K281/189*f*
Piano sonata, E♭ major (1775)	K282/189*g*
Piano sonata, G major (1775)	K283/189*h*
Canon, 4 in 2, F major (1787)	K283/515*b*
Piano sonata, D major (1775)	K284/205*b*
Arrangement of J. B. Wendling's concerto (1777)	K284*e*
Rondo (1777)	K284*f*
Flute quartet, D major (1777)	K285

K285*a*	Flute quartet, G major (1777–8)
K286/269*a*	Notturno, D major (1776–7)
K287/271*H*	Divertimento, B♭ major (1777)
K288/246*c*	Allegro, F major (1776)
K289/271*g*	Divertimento, E♭ major (1777)
K290/167*AB*	March, D major (1772)
K292/196*c*	Sonata (Duo), B♭ major (1775)
K293*e*	Cara la dolce fiamma (1778)
K294	Alcandro, lo confesso . . .
	Non sò d'onde viene (1778)
KA294*d*/516*f*	Musikalisches Würfelspiel, C major (1787)
K295	Se al labbro mio non credi (1778)
K296	Violin and piano sonata, C major (1778)
K296*b*	12 contredanses (1776)
K297/300*a*	Symphony No. 31, 'Paris', D major (1778)
K298	Flute quartet, A major (1786–7)
K299/297*c*	Flute concerto, harp, C major (1778)
K300	[Gavotte], B♭ major (1778)
K301/293*a*	Violin and piano sonata, G major (1778)
K302/293*b*	Violin and piano sonata, E♭ major (1778)
K303/293*c*	Violin and piano sonata, C major (1778)
K304/300*c*	Violin and piano sonata, E minor (1778)
K305/293*d*	Violin and piano sonata, A major (1778)
K306/300*l*	Violin and piano sonata, D major (1778)

Oiseaux, si tous les ans, C major (1777–8)	K307/284*d*
Dans un bois solitaire, A♭ major (1777–8)	K308/295*b*
Piano sonata, C major (1777)	K309/284*b*
Piano sonata, A minor (1778)	K310/300*d*
Piano sonata, D major (1777)	K311/284*c*
Allegro, G minor (1789–90)	K312/590*d*
Flute concerto, G major (1778)	K313/285*c*
Flute concerto, D major (1778)	K314/285*d*
Andante, C major (1779–80)	K315/285*e*
8 minuets (1773)	K315*a*/315*g*
Popoli di Tessaglia . . . Io non chiedo (1779)	K316/300*b*
Missa, 'Coronation', C major (1779)	K317
Symphony No. 32, G major (1779)	K318
Symphony No. 33, B♭ major (1779)	K319
Serenade, 'Posthorn' D major (1779)	K320
Vesperae de Dominica, C major (1779)	K321
Kyrie, E♭ major (1778)	K322/296*a*
Kyrie, C major (1787–9)	K323/A15
Church sonata No. 15, C major (1779)	K328/317*c*
Church sonata No. 16, C major (1779)	K329/317*a*
Piano sonata, C major (1781–3)	K330/300*h*
Piano sonata, A major (1781–3)	K331/300*i*
Piano sonata, F major (1781–3)	K332/300*k*
Piano sonata, B♭ major (1783–4)	K333/315*c*

K334/320*b*	Divertimento, D major (1779–80)
K335/320*a*	Two marches, D major (1779)
K336/336*d*	Church sonata No. 17, C major (1780)
K337	Missa solemnis, C major (1780)
K338	Symphony No. 34, C major (1780)
K339	Vesperae solennes de confessore, C major (1780)
K341/368*a*	Kyrie, D minor (1780–1)
K343,*i*/336*c,i*	O Gottes Lamm, F major (1787)
K343,*ii*/336*c,ii*	Als aus Ägypten, C major (1787)
K344/336*b*	Zaide (1780)
K345/336*a*	Thamos, König in Ägypten (1776–9)
K346/439*a*	Luci care, luci belle (1783–6)
K347/382*f*	Wo der perlende Wein im Glase blinkt, D major (?1782)
K348/382*g*	V'amo di core teneramente, G major (?1782)
K349/367*a*	Die Zufriedenheit: Was frag ich viel, G major (1780–81)
K351/367*b*	Komm, liebe Zither, C major (1780–81)
K352/374*c*	8 variations, F major (1781)
K353/300*f*	12 variations, E♭ major (1781–2)
K354/299*a*	12 variations, E♭ major (1778)
K355/576*b*	Minuet, D major (?1786–7)
K356/617*a*	Adagio, C major (1791)
K358/186*c*	Sonata, B♭ major (1773–4)
K359/374*a*	12 variations, G major (1781)
K360/374*b*	6 variations, G minor (1781)

Serenade for 13 wind instruments, B♭ major (1781–4)	K361/370*a*
March, C major (1780–1)	K362
3 minuets (1782–3)	K363
Sinfonia concertante, E♭ major (1779)	K364/320*d*
Concerto, No. 10, 2 pianos, E♭ major (1779)	K365/316*a*
Idomeneo (1781)	K366
Ballet music for Idomeneo (1781)	K367
Ma che vi fece . . . Sperai vicino (1779–80)	K368
Misera! dove son . . . Ah! non son'io (1781)	K369
Oboe quartet, F major (1781)	K370/368*b*
Rondo, E♭ major (1781)	K371
Violin and piano sonata, B♭ major (1781)	K372
Rondo, C major (1781)	K373
A questo seno . . . Or che il cielo (1781)	K374
Serenade for wind instruments, E♭ major (1781)	K375
Violin and piano sonata, F major (1781)	K376/374*d*
Violin and piano sonata, F major (1781)	K377/374*e*
Violin and piano sonata, B♭ major (1779–81)	K378/317*d*
Violin and piano sonata, G major (1781)	K379/373*a*
Violin and piano sonata, E♭ major (1781)	K380/374*f*
Sonata for 2 pianos, D major (1772)	K381/123*a*
Rondo, D major (1782)	K382
Nehmt meinen Dank (1782)	K383
Die Entführung aus dem Serail (1782)	K384

K385	Symphony No. 35, 'Haffner', D major (1782)
K386	Rondo, A major (1782)
K387	'Haydn' quartet No. 14, G major (1782)
K388/384*a*	Serenade for wind instruments, C minor (1782–3)
K389/384*A*	Welch ängstliches Beben (1782)
K390/340*c*	An die Hoffnung:
	Ich würd,auf meinem Pfad, D minor (1781–2)
K391/340*b*	An die Einsamkeit: Sei du mein Trost, B♭ major (1781–2)
K392/340*a*	Verdankt sei es dem Glanz der Grossen, F major (1781–2)
K393/385*b*	Solfeggios for voice (1782)
K393/385*n*	Fugue a 4, A major (1782)
K394/383*a*	Prelude and Fugue, C major (1782)
K395/300*g*	Capriccio, C major (1777)
K396/385*f*	Sonata movement, C minor (1782)
K397/385*g*	Fantasia, D minor (1782–7)
K398/416*e*	6 variations in F major (1783)
K399/385*i*	Suite, C major (1782)
K400/372*a*	Allegro, B♭ major (1781)
K401/375*e*	Fugue, G minor (1772)
K402/385*e*	Violin and piano sonata, A major (1782)
K403/385*c*	Violin and piano sonata, C major (1782)
K404/385*d*	Sonata, C major (?1782 or c.1788)
K405	Arrangement of J. S. Bach's 5 fugues (1782)
K406/516*b*	String quintet No. 4, C minor (1788)

K428/421*b*	'Haydn' quartet No. 16, E♭ major (1783)
K429/468*a*	Dir, Seele des Weltalls (1785)
K430/424*a*	Lo sposo deluso (?1784)
K431/425*b*	Misero! o sogno . . .
	Aura, che intorno spiri (1783)
K432/421*a*	Così dunque tradisci . . .
	Aspri rimorsi atroci (?1783)
K433/416*c*	Männer suchen stets zu naschen (1783)
K434/480*b*	Del gran regno delle amazzoni (1785)
K435/416*b*	Müsst'ich auch durch tausend Drachen (1783)
K436	Ecco quel fiero istante (1783–6)
K437	Mi lagnerò tacendo (1783–6)
K438	Se lontan, ben mio, tu sei (1783–6)
K439	Due pupille amabili (1783–6)
K440/383*b*	In te spero, o sposo amata (1782)
K441	Das Bandel: Liebes Mandel, wo is's Bandel? (?1783)
K442	Piano trio, D minor (?1783–90)
K443/404*b*	Fugue a 3, G major (?1782)
K444/425*a*	Adagio maestoso, G major (1783)
K445/320*c*	March, D major (1780)
K446/416*d*	Pantalon und Colombine (1783)
K447	Horn concerto, E♭ major (1784–7)
K448/375*a*	Sonata for 2 pianos, D major (1781)
K449	Piano concerto No. 14, E♭ major (1784)

Piano concerto No. 15, B♭ major (1784)	**K450**
Piano concerto No. 16, D major (1784)	**K451**
Piano quintet, E♭ major (1784)	**K452**
Piano concerto No. 17, G major (1784)	**K453**
Kleiner Trauermarsch, C minor (1784)	**K453***a*
Exercise book for Barbara Ployer	453*b*
Violin and piano sonata, B♭ major (1784)	**K454**
10 variations, G major (1784)	**K455**
Piano concerto No. 18, B♭ major (1784)	**K456**
Piano sonata, C minor (1784)	**K457**
'Haydn' quartet No. 17, 'Hunt', B♭ major (1784)	**K458**
Piano concerto No. 19, F major (1784)	**K459**
2 variations, A major (1784)	**K460/454***a*
6 minuets (1784)	**K461/448***a*
6 contredanses (1784)	**K462/448***b*
2 minuets with contredanses (1784)	**K463/448***c*
'Haydn' quartet No, 18, A major (1785)	**K464**
'Haydn' quartet No. 19, 'Dissonance', C major (1785)	**K465**
Piano concerto No. 20, D minor (1785)	**K466**
Piano concerto No. 21, C major (1785)	**K467**
Gesellenreise:	**K468**
Die ihr einem neuen Grade, B♭ major (1785)	
Davide penitente (1785)	**K469**
Andante, A major (1785)	**K470**

K470*a*	Arrangement of G. B. Viotti's, Violin concerto No. 16 (1785)
K471	Die Maurerfreude (1785)
K472	Der Zauberer: Ihr Mädchen, flieht Damöten ja!, G minor (1785)
K473	Die Zufriedenheit: Wie sanft, wie ruhig, B♭ major (1785)
K474	Die betrogene Welt: Der reiche Tor, G major (1785)
K475	Fantasia, C minor (1785)
K476	Das Veilchen, G major (1785)
K477/479*a*	Maurerische Trauermusik, C minor (1785)
K478	Piano quartet, G minor (1785)
K479	Dite almeno, in che mancai (1785)
K480	Mandina amabile (1785)
K481	Violin and piano sonata, E♭ major (1785)
K482	Piano concerto No. 22, E♭ major (1785)
K483	Zerfliesset heut', geliebte Brüder, B♭ major (1785)
K484	Ihr unsre neuen Leiter, G major (1785)
K845	Rondo, D major (1786)
K485*a*/506*a*	Attwood Studies (1785–6)
K486	Der Schauspieldirektor (1786)
K486*a*/295*a*	Basta, vincesti . . . Ah, non lasciarmi (1778)
K487/496*a*	12 duos (1785)
K488	Piano concerto No. 23, A major (1786)
K489	Spiegarti non poss'io (1786)
K490	Venga la morte . . . Non temer, amato bene (1786)
K491	Piano concerto No. 24, C minor (1786)

K512	Alcandro, lo confesso . . . Non sò d'onde viene (1787)
K513	Mentre ti lascio, o figlia (1787)
K514/386*b*	Rondo, D major (1791)
K515	String quintet No. 2, C major (1787)
K516	String quintet No. 3, G minor (1787)
K516*f*	Musikalisches Würfelspiel (1787)
K517	Die Alte: Zu meiner Zeit, E minor (1787)
K518	Die Verschweigung:
	Sobald Damötas Chloen sieht, F major (1787)
K519	Das Lied der Trennung:
	Die Engel Gottes weinen, F minor (1787)
K520	Als Luise die Briefe, C major (1787)
K521	Sonata, C major (1787)
K522	A Musical Joke, F major (1787)
K523	Abendempfindung, F major (1787)
K524	An Chloe:
	Wenn die Lieb'aus deinen blauen, E♭ major (1787)
K525	Eine kleine Nachtmusik, G major (1787)
K526	Violin and piano sonata, A major (1787)
K527	Don Giovanni (1787)
K528	Bella mia fiamma . . . Resta, o cara (1787)
K529	Des kleinen Friedrichs Geburtstag:
	Es war einmal, ihr Leutchen, F major (1787)
K530	Das Traumbild: Wo bist du, Bild, E♭ major (1787)

K550	Symphony No. 40, G minor (1788)	
K551	Symphony No. 41, 'Jupiter', C major (1788)	
K552	Beim Auszug in das Feld:	
	Dem hohen Kaiser-Worte treu, A major (1788)	
K553	Alleluia, C major (1788)	
K554	Ave Maria, F major (1788)	
K555	Lacrimoso son'io, A minor (1788)	
K556	G'rechtelt's enk, G major (1788)	
K557	Nascoso è il mio sol, F minor (1788)	
K558	Gehn wir im Prater, B♭ major (1788)	
K559	Difficile lectu mihi Mars, F major (1788)	
K560a	O du eselhafter Peierl!, 4 in 1, F major (1788)	
K561	Bona nox, bist a rechta Ox, A major (1788)	
K562	Caro bell'idol mio, A major (1788)	
K562a	Canon, B♭ major	
K563	'Divertimento', String trio, E♭ major (1788)	
K564	Piano trio, G major (1788)	
K565	2 Contredanses (1788)	
K566	Arrangement of G. F. Handel's Acis and Galatea (1788)	
K567	6 German Dances (1788)	
K568	12 minuets (1788)	
K569	Ohne Zwang, aus eignem Triebe (1789)	
K570	Piano sonata, B♭ major (1789)	
K571	6 German dances (1789)	

Arrangement of Handel's Messiah (1789)	K572
9 variations, D major (1789)	K573
Kleine Gigue, G major (1789)	K574
'Prussian' quartet No. 21, D major (1789)	K575
Piano sonata, D major (1789)	K576
Grunse alfin il momento . . . Al desio di chi ch'adora (1789)	K577
Alma grande e nobil core (1789)	K578
Un moto di gioia mi sento (1789)	K579
Schon lacht der holde Frühling (1789)	K580
Clarinet quintet, A major (1789)	K581
Chi sà, chi sà qual sia (1789)	K582
Vado, ma dove? oh Dei! (1789)	K583
Rivolgete a lui lo sguardo (1789)	K584
12 minuets (1789)	K585
12 German dances (1789)	K586
Contredanse, 'Der Sieg vom Helden Coburg', C major (1789)	K587
Così fan tutte (1790)	K588
'Prussian' quartet No. 22, B♭ major (1790)	K589
'Prussian' quartet No. 23, F major (1790)	K590
Arrangement of Handel's Alexander's Feast (1790)	K591
Arrangement of Handel's Ode for St Cecilia's Day (1790)	K592
String quintet No. 5, D major (1790)	K593
Adagio and Allegro, F minor (1790)	K594
Piano concerto No. 27, B♭ major (1791)	K595

K596	Sehnsucht nach dem Frühling:
	Komm, Lieber Mai, F major (1791)
K597	Im Frühlingsanfang:
	Erwacht zum neuen Leben, E♭ major (1791)
K598	Das Kinderspiel: Wir Kinder, A major (1791)
K599	6 minuets (1791)
K600	6 German Dances (1791)
K601	4 minuets (1791)
K602	4 German dances (1791)
K603	2 contredanses (1791)
K604	2 minuets (1791)
K605	3 German dances (1791)
K606	6 Ländler (1791)
K607/605a	Contredanse, 'Il trionfo delle dame', E♭ major (1791)
K608	Orgelstück (Fantasia) für eine Uhr, F minor (1791)
K609	5 contredanses, 'Non più andrai' (1787–8)
K610	Contredanse, 'Les filles malicieuses', G major (1791)
K611	German dance, 'Die Leyerer', C major (1791)
K612	Per questa bella mano, B major (1791)
K613	8 variations, F major (1791)
K614	String quintet No. 6, E♭ major (1791)
K615	Viviano felici (1791)
K616	Andante für eine Walze in eine kleine Orgel, F major (1791)
K617	Adagio and Rondo, C minor (1791)

mozart

recommended recordings

The following list of recordings is included as a guide to some of the interpretations of Mozart's work available at the time of writing and is by no means intended as an exhaustive catalogue. The works are listed first, followed by details of the recording: the artists, record company and disc number. All numbers given are those that apply to the compact disc format, but many recordings can also be bought on conventional tape cassette.

K364/K320*d*[1]	SINFONIA CONCERTANTE IN E♭ MAJOR
K190/K186*E*[2]	CONCERTONE IN C MAJOR FOR TWO VIOLINS,
	OBOE, CELLO AND ORCHESTRA

[1]Perlman, Zukerman.[2]Jouval, Bergman. Israel Philharmonic Orch., Mehta.
DG 415 486-2GH.

K364/320*d*[1]	SINFONIA CONCERTANTE IN E♭ MAJOR
KA9/297*b*	SINFONIA CONCERTANTE IN E♭ MAJOR

[1]Phillips, Gallagher. [2]Dibner, Purvis, Singer, Taylor OCO.
DG 429 784-2GH.

KA9/K297*b*[1]	SINFONIA CONCERTANTE IN E♭ MAJOR
K407/386*c*[2]	HORN QUINTET IN E♭ MAJOR
K452[3]	QUINTET IN E♭ MAJOR FOR PIANO AND WIND

[1]Gatt, Hill, Wickens, ECO,Tuckwell.
[2]Members of Gabrieli Quartet, Tuckwell.
[3]Gatt, Hill, Ogdon, Tuckwell, Wickens.
Decca 421 393-2DH.

CLARINET CONCERTO IN A MAJOR   K622[1]
CLARINET QUINTET IN A MAJOR   K581[2]
[1]King, ECO, Tate.
[2]King, Gabrieli Str Quartet. Hyperion CDA66199.

FLUTE CONCERTO NO. 1 IN G MAJOR   K313/285*c*
ANDANTE IN C MAJOR   K315/285*e*
FLUTE AND HARP CONCERTO IN C MAJOR   K299/297*c*[1]
[1]Allen. Palma, OCO. DG 427 677-2GH.

HORN CONCERTOS
NO. 1 IN D MAJOR   K412
NO. 2 IN E♭ MAJOR   K417
NO. 3 IN E♭ MAJOR   K447
NO. 4 IN E♭ MAJOR   K495
Brain, Philharmonia Orch., von Karajan.
EMI mono CDH7 61013-2.

HORN CONCERTOS
NO. 1 IN D MAJOR   K412
NO. 2 IN E♭ MAJOR   K417
NO. 3 IN E♭ MAJOR   K447
NO. 4 IN E♭ MAJOR   K495
ECO, Tuckwell. Decca 410 284-2DH.

K314/285*d*	OBOE CONCERTO IN C MAJOR
	Boyd; COE, Berglund.
	ASV CDCOE808.

PIANO CONCERTOS

K37	NO. 1 IN F MAJOR
K39	NO. 2 IN B♭ MAJOR
K40	NO. 3 IN D MAJOR
K41	NO. 4 IN G MAJOR
K175	NO. 5 IN D MAJOR
K238	NO. 6 IN B♭ MAJOR
K246	NO. 8 IN C MAJOR
K271	NO. 9 IN E♭ MAJOR
K413/387*a*	NO. 11 IN F MAJOR
K414/385*p*	NO. 12 IN A MAJOR
K415/387*b*	NO. 13 IN C MAJOR
K449	NO. 14 IN E♭ MAJOR
K450	NO. 15 IN B♭ MAJOR
K451	NO. 16 IN D MAJOR
K453	NO. 17 IN G MAJOR
K456	NO. 18 IN B♭ MAJOR
K459	NO. 19 IN F MAJOR
K466	NO. 20 IN D MINOR
K467	NO. 21 IN C MAJOR
K482	NO. 22 IN E♭ MAJOR

No. 23 in A major	K488	
No. 24 in C minor	K491	
No. 25 in C major	K503	
No. 26 in D major, 'Coronation'	K537	
No. 27 in B♭ major	K595	
Rondo in D major	K382	

ECO, Barenboim. EMI CZS7 62825-2.

PIANO CONCERTOS

No. 15 in B♭ major	K450
No. 16 in D major	K451

ECO, Perahia. CBS Masterworks CD37824.

PIANO CONCERTOS

No. 20 in D minor	K466
No. 27 in B♭ major	K595
No. 11 in E major	K413
No. 12 in A major	K414
No. 14 in E♭ major	K449

ECO, Perahia. CBS Masterworks CD42241 and CD42243.

PIANO CONCERTOS

No. 20 in D minor	K466
No. 21 in C major	K467

Uchida, ECO, Tate. Philips 416 381-2PH.

PIANO CONCERTOS

K467[1]	NO. 21 IN C MAJOR
K482	NO. 22 IN E♭ MAJOR
K488	NO. 23 IN A MAJOR
K491[2]	NO. 24 IN C MINOR
K537	NO. 26 IN D MAJOR, 'CORONATION'
K595	NO. 27 IN B♭ MAJOR
K365	CONCERTO FOR TWO PIANOS IN E♭ MAJOR

R Casadesus, [1]G Casadesus; [2]Cleveland Orch., Columbia Symphony Orch., Szell; [1]Philadelphia Orch., Ormandy. Sony CD46519.

PIANO CONCERTOS

K467	NO. 21 IN C MAJOR
K503	NO. 25 IN C MAJOR

Kovacevich, LSO, Davis. Philips 426 077-2PC.

PIANO CONCERTOS

K482	NO. 22 IN E♭ MAJOR
K488	NO. 23 IN A MAJOR

ECO, Barenboim. EMI CDM7 69122-2.

PIANO CONCERTOS

K488	NO. 23 IN A MAJOR
K491	NO. 24 IN C MINOR

Curzon, LSO, Kertész. Decca 430 497-2DWO.

DOUBLE PIANO CONCERTO, E♭ MAJOR	K365/316a[1]
DOUBLE PIANO CONCERTO, F MAJOR, 'LODRON'	K242[2]
ANDANTE AND VARIATIONS IN G MAJOR	K501
FANTASIA IN F MINOR (ARR. BUSONI)	K608

Perahia, Lupu, [1]ECO. Sony Classical CD44915.

VIOLIN CONCERTOS

NO. 3 IN G MAJOR	K216
NO. 4 IN D MAJOR	K218
NO. 5 IN A MAJOR	K219

Altenburger, German Bach Soloists, Winscherman. LaserLight 15 525.

SERENADE IN B♭ MAJOR FOR 13 WIND INSTRUMENTS	K361/370a

ASMF Wind Ensemble, Marriner. Philips 412 726-2PH.

SERENADE IN D MAJOR 'HAFFNER'	K250/248b

Suk, Prague Chamber Orch., Hlaváček.
Supraphon Gems 2SUP0006.

SERENADE IN D MAJOR 'HAFFNER'	K250/248b[1]
MARCH IN D MAJOR 'HAFFNER'	K249

[1]Brown, ASMF, Marriner. Philips 416154-2PH.

WIND SERENADES

| K375 | E♭ major |
| K388/384*a* | C minor |

Wind soloists of the COE, Schneider. ASV CDCOE802.

DIVERTIMENTOS

| K287/271*b* | B♭ major |
| K205/167*a* | D major |

Salzburg Mozarteum Camerata Academica, Végh. Capriccio 10 271.

K205/167*a*[1]	DIVERTIMENTO, D MAJOR
K334/320*b*[2]	DIVERTIMENTO, D MAJOR
K290/167*ab*[1]	MARCH IN D MAJOR

Franz Liszt Chamber Orch.[1]Rolla, [2]Sándor.
Hung. HRC080.

K63	CASSATION, G MAJOR
K99/63*a*	CASSATION, B♭ MAJOR
K546	ADAGIO AND FUGUE IN C MINOR

Salzburg Camerata, Végh. Capriccio 10 192.

ORCHESTRAL WORKS

K185/167*a*[1]	SERENADE IN D MAJOR
K189/167*b*	MARCH IN D MAJOR
K609	FIVE CONTREDANSES

NOTTURNO IN D MAJOR — K286/269*a*

¹Engegard (vn), Salzburg Mozarteum Camerata Academica, Végh.
Capriccio 10 302.

FIVE MINUETS	K461/448*a*[1]
SIX CONTREDANSES	K462/448*b*[1]
CONTREDANSE, 'DAS DONNERWETTER' D MAJOR	K534[1]
CONTREDANSE, 'LA BATAILLE' C MAJOR	K535[1]
CONTREDANSE, 'DER SIEG VOM HELDEN KOBURG' C MAJOR	K587[1]
TWO CONTREDANSES	K603[1]
TWO MINUETS WITH CONTREDANSES (QUADRILLES)	K463/448*c*

GERMAN DANCES[1]

SIX	K509
SIX	K600
THREE	K605

MARCHES[1]

D MAJOR	K52
D MAJOR	K189/167*b*
C MAJOR	K214
D MAJOR	K215/213*b*
D MAJOR	K237/189*c*
F MAJOR	K248
D MAJOR	K249

K335/320*a*	TWO IN D MAJOR
K408,*i*/383*e*	C MAJOR
K408,*ii*/385*a*	D MAJOR
K408,*iii*/383*f*	C MAJOR
K445/320*c*	D MAJOR

OVERTURES

K620	DIE ZAUBERFLÖTE
K492	LE NOZZE DI FIGARO
K111	ASCANIO IN ALBA
K366	IDOMENEO
K486	DER SCHAUSPIELDIREKTOR
K588	COSÌ FAN TUTTE
K384	DIE ENTFÜHRUNG AUS DEM SERAIL
K196	LA FINTA GIARDINIERA
K135	LUCIO SILLA
K621	LA CLEMENZA DI TITO
K527	DON GIOVANNI
	IDOMENEO MARCHES [1] NOS. 8, 14 AND 25
	LE NOZZE DI FIGARO MARCH NO. 23

Staatskapelle Dresden, Vonk.

[1]Salzburg Mozarteum Orch., Graf. Capriccio 10 809.

| K525 | SERENADE IN G MAJOR 'EINE KLEINE NACHTMUSIK' |
| K366 | IDOMENEO, OVERTURE |

Die Entführung aus dem Serail, overture	K384
Der Schauspieldirektor, overture	K486
Le nozze di Figaro, overture	K492
Don Giovanni, overture	K527
Così fan tutte, overture	K588
La clemenza di Tito, overture	K621
Die Zauberflöte, overture	K620

Tafelmusik, Weil. Sony CD46695.

SYMPHONIES

No. 1 in E♭ major	K16
No. 4 in D major	K19
No. 5 in B♭ major	K22
No. 6 in F major	K43
No. 55 in B♭ major	KA214/45*b*
No. 7 in D major	K45
No. 8 in D major	K48
No. 9 in C major	K73/75*a*
No. 44 in D major	K81/73*l*
No. 47 in D major	K97/73*m*
No. 45 in D major	K95/73*n*
No. 11 in D major	K84/73*q*
No. 10 in G major	K74/73*p*
No. 46 in C major	K96/111*b*
No. 42 in F major	K75

K110/75*b*	No. 12 IN G MAJOR
K112	No. 13 IN F MAJOR
	Prague Chamber Orch., Mackerras
	Telarc CD80256 CD80272/3.

SYMPHONIES

K183/173*dB*	No. 25 IN G MINOR
K184/161*a*	No. 26 IN E♭ MAJOR
K201/186*a*	No. 29 IN A MAJOR
	English Concert, Pinnock (hpd).
	Archiv Produktion 431 679-2.

SYMPHONIES

K199/161*b*	No. 27 IN G MAJOR
K200/189*k*	No. 28 IN C MAJOR
K338	No. 34 IN C MAJOR
	English Sinfonia, Groves.
	Pickwick IMP Classics PCD933.

SYMPHONIES

K201/186*a*	No. 29 IN A MAJOR
K318	No. 32 IN G MAJOR
K319	No. 33 IN B♭ MAJOR
	English Sinfonia, Groves.
	Pickwick IMP Classics PCD922.

SYMPHONIES

No. 29 IN A MAJOR   K201/186*a*

No. 33 IN B♭ MAJOR   K319

EBS, Gardiner. Philips 412 736-2PH.

SYMPHONIES

No. 31 IN D MAJOR 'PARIS', (FIRST VERSION)   K297/300*a*

No. 34 IN C MAJOR   K338

EBS, Gardiner. Philips 420 937-2PH.

SYMPHONIES

No. 31 IN D MAJOR 'PARIS'   K297/300*a*

No. 38 IN D MAJOR 'PRAGUE'   K504

English Sinfonia, Groves. Pickwick IMP Classics PCD892.

SYMPHONIES

No. 35 IN D MAJOR 'HAFFNER'   K385[1]

No. 36 IN C MAJOR 'LINZ'   K425[1]

RONDO FOR VIOLIN AND ORCHESTRA IN B♭ MAJOR   K269/261*a*[2]

[1]Bavarian Radio Symphony Orch., Kubelík.

[2]Saint Paul Chamber Orch., Pinchas Zukerman (vn).

CBS Masterworks CD44647.

SYMPHONIES

K425　　No. 36 IN C MAJOR 'LINZ'
K504　　No. 38 IN D MAJOR 'PRAGUE'
　　　　ECO, Tate. EMI CDC7 47442-2.

SYMPHONIES

K543　　No. 39 IN E♭ MAJOR
K551　　No. 41 IN C MAJOR 'JUPITER'
　　　　Staatskapelle Dresden, Davis. Philips 410 046-2PH.

SYMPHONIES

K543　　No. 39 IN E♭ MAJOR
K551　　No. 41 IN C MAJOR 'JUPITER'
　　　　London Classical Players, Norrington. EMI CDC7 54090-2.

SYMPHONIES

K550　　No. 40 IN G MINOR
K551　　No. 41 IN C MAJOR 'JUPITER'
　　　　ECO, Tate. EMI CDC7 47147-2.

SYMPHONIES

K550　　No. 40 IN G MINOR
K551　　No. 41 IN C MAJOR 'JUPITER'
　　　　Prague Chamber Orch. Mackerras.
　　　　Telarc CD80139.

17 Church Sonatas
Watson (org), King's Consort, King (org). Hyperion CDA66377.

COMPLETE EDITION VOLUME 14 PIANO QUINTET, QUARTETS, TRIOS, ETC.

QUINTET IN E♭ MAJOR FOR PIANO AND WIND	K452[1]
CLARINET TRIO IN E♭ MAJOR 'KEGELSTATT'	K498[2]
ADAGIO AND RONDO IN C MINOR	K617[3]
ADAGIO IN C MAJOR	K356/617a[4]

PIANO QUARTETS[5]

G MINOR	K478
E♭ MAJOR	K493

PIANO TRIOS[6]

B♭ MAJOR	K254
D MINOR (CPTED. STADLER AND MARGUERRE)	K442
G MAJOR	K496
B♭ MAJOR	K502
E MAJOR	K542
C MAJOR	K548
G MAJOR	K564

[1]Nicolet (fl), [13]Holliger (ob), [1]Brunner & [2]Brymer (cls), [1]Baumann (hn), [1]Thunemann (bn), [34]Hoffmann (glass harmonica), [2]Ireland, [3]Schouten, [3]Giuranna (vas), [3]Decroos (vc), [56]Beaux Arts Trio (Cohen vn, Greenhouse vc, Pressler pf), [1]Brendel, [2]Kovacevich (pfs) Philips 422 514-2PME5.

COMPLETE EDITION VOLUME 11

STRING QUINTETS

K174	B♭ MAJOR
K406/516*b*	C MINOR
K515	C MAJOR
K516	G MINOR
K593	D MAJOR
K614	E♭ MAJOR

Grumiaux, Gérecz (vns); Janzer, Lesueur (vas); Czako (vc).
Philips 422 511-2PME3.

'PRUSSIAN' STRING QUARTETS

K575	D MAJOR
K590	F MAJOR

Salomon Quartet. Hyperion CDA66355.

'HAYDN' STRING QUARTETS

K387	G MAJOR
K421/417*b*	D MINOR

Bartók Quartet. Hung HRC129.

'HAYDN' STRING QUARTETS

K421/417*b*	D MINOR
K465	C MAJOR 'DISSONANCE'

Salomon Quartet. Hyperion CDA66170

'HAYDN' STRING QUARTETS

G MAJOR	K387
D MINOR	K421/417*b*
E♭ MAJOR	K428/421*b*
B♭ MAJOR 'HUNT'	K458
A MAJOR	K464
C MAJOR 'DISSONANCE'	K465

Chilingirian Quartet. CRD CRD3362/4.

FLUTE QUARTETS

D MAJOR	K285
G MAJOR	K285*a*
C MAJOR	KA171/285*b*
A MAJOR	K298

Bennett (fl); Grumiaux Trio. Philips 422 835-2PC.

DIVERTIMENTO IN E♭ MAJOR FOR STRING TRIO	K563
SIX PRELUDES AND FUGUES (AFTER BACH)	K404*a*
NO. 1 IN D MINOR	
NO. 2 IN G MINOR	
NO. 3 IN F MAJOR	

Grumiaux Trio. Philips 416 485-2PH.

K563	DIVERTIMENTO IN E♭ MAJOR FOR STRING TRIO
K423	DUO FOR VIOLIN AND VIOLA G MAJOR
K424	DUO FOR VIOLIN AND VIOLA B♭ MAJOR

Kovács (vn), Németh (va), Banda (vc).

Hung. HRC072.

COMPLETE EDITION VOLUME 18

PIANO VARIATIONS, RONDOS, ETC.

VARIATIONS

K24[1]	G MAJOR
K25[1]	D MAJOR
K179/189a[1]	C MAJOR
K180/173c[1]	G MAJOR
K264/315d[1]	C MAJOR
K265/300e[1]	C MAJOR
K352/374c[31]	F MAJOR
K353/300f[1]	E♭ MAJOR
K354/299a[1]	E♭ MAJOR
K398/416e[1]	F MAJOR
K455[1]	G MAJOR
K460/454a[1]	A MAJOR
K500[1]	B♭ MAJOR
K573[1]	D MAJOR
K613[1]	F MAJOR

MINUETS

F MAJOR	K1*d*[5]
G MAJOR/C MAJOR	K1/1e/1*f*[5]
F MAJOR	K2[5]
F MAJOR	K4[5]
F MAJOR	K5[5]
D MAJOR	K94/73*b*[5]
D MAJOR	K355/576*b*[2]
FANTASIA IN D MINOR	K397/385*g*[2]

RONDOS

D MAJOR	K485[2]
A MINOR	K511[2]
ADAGIO IN B MINOR	K540[2]
GIGUE IN G MAJOR	K574[2]
KLAVIERSTÜCK IN F MAJOR	K33*b*[3]
CAPRICCIO IN C MAJOR	K395/300*g*[3]
MARCH NO. 1 IN C MAJOR	K408/383*e*[3]
PRELUDE AND FUGUE IN C MAJOR	K394/383*a*[3]

ALLEGROS

C MAJOR	K1*b*[3]
F MAJOR	K1*c*[3]
B♭ MAJOR	K3[3]
C MAJOR	K5*a*[3]

K312/590d[5]	**G minor**
K400/372a[3]	**B♭ major (cpted Stadler)**
K399/385i[3]	**Suite in C major**
K453a[3]	**Kleine Trauermarsch in C minor**
K1a[3]	**Andante in C major**
K401/375e[3]	**Fugue in G minor**

[1]Haebler & [2]Uchida (pfs), [3]Koopman (hpd). Philips 422 518-2PME5.

K448/375a	**Double Piano Sonata in D major**
(D940	**with Schubert. Fantasia in F minor)**

Perahia & Lupu (pfs). CBS Masterworks CD39511.

PIANO WORKS

K265/300e	**Variations on 'Ah, vous dirai-je, maman'**
K616	**Andante in F major**
K511	**Rondo in A minor**
K356/617a	**Adagio in C major**
K355/576b	**Minuet in D major**
K574	**Gigue in G major**
K540	**Adagio in B minor**
K455	**Variations on 'Unser dummer Pöbel meint'**

Schiff. Decca. 421 369-2DH.

COMPLETE EDITION VOLUME 17

PIANO SONATAS

C MAJOR	K279/189*d*
F MAJOR	K280/189*e*
B♭ MAJOR	K281/189*f*
E♭ MAJOR	K282/189*g*
G MAJOR	K283/189*h*
D MAJOR	K284/205*b*
C MAJOR	K309/284*b*
A MINOR	K310/300*d*
D MAJOR	K311/284*c*
C MAJOR	K330/300*h*
A MAJOR	K331/300*i*
F MAJOR	K332/300*k*
B♭ MAJOR	K333/315*c*
C MINOR	K457
F MAJOR	K533/494
C MAJOR	K545
B♭ MAJOR	K570
D MAJOR	K576
FANTASIA IN C MINOR	K475

Uchida (pf). Philips 422 517-2PME5.

MASONIC MUSIC

K148/125*b*[15]	LOBEGESANG AUF DIE FEIERLICHE JOHANNISLOGE
K429/K468*a*[136]	DIR, SEELE DES WELTALLS
K468[15]	LIED ZUR GESELLENREISE
K471[136]	DIE MAURERFREUDE
K477/479*a*[6]	MAURERISCHE TRAUERMUSIK
K483[134]	ZERFLIESSET HEUT', GELIEBTE BRÜDER
K484[134]	IHR UNSRE NEUEN LEITER
K619[15]	DIE IHR DES UNERMESSLICHEN WELTALLS
K623[1236]	LAUT VERKÜNDE UNSRE FREUDE
K623a[34]	LASST UNS MIT GESCHLUNGNEN HÄNDEN

[1]Krenn (ten), [2]Krause (bar), [3]Edinburgh Festival Ch.,
Fischer ([4]org/[5]pf), [6]LSO, Kertész.
Decca Serenata 425 722-2DM.

MOZART (ED. MAUNDER)

K427/417*a* MISSA IN C MINOR

Auger, Dawson (sops), Ainsley (ten), Thomas (bass),
Winchester Cathedral Ch., Winchester College Quiristers, AAM, Hogwood.
O-L 425 528-2OH.

K626 MOZART (CPTD SÜSSMAYR)
REQUIEM IN D MINOR

McNair (sop), Watkinson (contr), Araiza
(ten), Lloyd (bass), ASMF, Marriner. Philips 432 087-2PH.

LIEDER

Abendempfindung	K523[2]
Als Luise die Briefe	K520[3]
An Chloe	K524[2]
Ch'io mi scordi di te . . . Non temer, amato bene	K505[2,3]
Dans un bois solitaire	K308/295b[2]
Ich würd, auf meinem Pfad	K390/340c[2]
Die ihr des unermesslichen Weltalls	K619[2]
Komm, liebe Zither, komm	K351/367b[1]
Das Lied der Trennung	K519[2]
Un moto di gioia	K579[2]
Oiseaux, si tous les ans	K307/284d[2]
Ridente la calma	K152/210a[2]
Sehnsucht nach dem Frühling	K596[2]
Sei du mein Trost	K391/340b[2]
Das Veilchen	K476[2]
Die Verschweigung	K518[2]
Der Zauberer	K472[2]
Die Zufriedenheit	K473[2]

Hendricks (sop), [1]Söllscher (gtr),
[2]Pires (pf), [3]Lausanne Chamber Orch., Eichenholz.
EMI CDC7 54007-2.

ARIAS

CONCERT ARIAS[1]

K505	CH'IO MI SCORDI DI TE
K583	VADO MA DOVE?
K578	ALMA GRANDE E NOBIL CORE
K383	NEHMT MEINEM DANK

K492	LE NOZZE DI FIGARO
	PORGI AMOR[2]
	E SUSANNA NON VIEN! . . . DOVE SONO[2]
	NON SO PIÙ[4]
	VOI CHE SAPETE[4]
	GIUNSE ALFIN IL MOMENTO . . . DEH VIENI, NON TRADAR[4]

K527	DON GIOVANNI
	AH, FUGGI IL TRADITOR[3]
	IN QUAL ECCESSI . . . MI TRADI QUELL'ALMA INGRATA[3]
	BATTI, BATTI, O BEL MASETTO[4]
	VEDRAI, CARINO[4]
	CRUDELE?... NON MI DIR[4]

K366	IDOMENEO
	ZEFFIRETTI LUSINGHIERI[4]

Schwarzkopf (sop), [1]LSO, [234]Philharmonia Orch., [23]Giulini, [4]Pritchard. EMI CDC7 47950-2

LE NOZZE DI FIGARO   K492

Taddei (bar), Moffo (sop), Waechter (bar),

Schwarzkopf (sop), Cossotto (mez), Gatta

(sop), Vinco (bass), Ercolani (ten), Cappuccilli (bass),

Fusco (sop), Philharmonia Chorus & Orch.,

Giulini. EMI CMS7 63266-2.

DON GIOVANNI   K527

Waechter (bar), Sutherland (sop),

Schwarzkopf (sop), Sciutti (sop), Alva (ten),

Taddei (bar), Cappuccilli (bar), Frick (bass), Philharmonia Chorus & Orch.,

Giulini. EMI CDS7 47260-8.

COMPLETE EDITION VOLUME 41

DON GIOVANNI   K527

Wixell (bar), Arroyo (sop), Te Kanawa (sop), Freni

(sop), Burrows (ten), Ganzarolli (bar), Van Allen (bass), Roni (bass),

Chorus & Orch. of the Royal Opera House, Covent Garden,

Davis. Philips 422 541-2PME3.

COSÌ FAN TUTTE   K588

Schwarzkopf (sop), Ludwig (mez), Steffek (sop), Kraus (ten),

Taddei (bar), Berry (bass), Philharmonia Chorus & Orch., Böhm.

EMI CMS7 69330-2.

K588 COSÌ FAN TUTTE

Mattila (sop), von Otter (mez), Szmytka (sop), Araiza (ten),
Allen (bar), van Dam (bass-bar), Ambrosian Opera Ch., ASM Fields, Marriner.
Philips 422 381-2PH3.

COMPLETE EDITION, VOLUME 26

K38 APOLLO ET HYACINTHUS

Wulkopf (mez), Mathis (sop), Johnson (ten), Auger (sop), Schwarz (mez),
Salzburg Chamber Ch., Salzburg Mozarteum Orch., Hager.
Philips 422 526-2PME2.

COMPLETE EDITION, VOLUME 28

K51 LA FINTA SEMPLICE

Hendricks (sop), Lorenz (bar), Johnson (sngr), Murray (mez), Lind (sop),
Blochwitz (ten), Schmidt (bar), CPE. Bach Chamber Orch., Schreier.
Philips 422 528-2PME2.

K384 DIE ENTFÜHRUNG AUS DEM SERAIL

Dawson (sop), Hirsti (sop), Heilmann (ten),
Gahmlich (ten), von Kannen (bass), Hinze (spkr), AAM, Hogwood.
O–L 430 339-2OH2.

LA CLEMENZA DI TITO   K621

Johnson (ten), Varady (sop), von Otter (mez),
Robbin (mez), McNair (sop), Hauptmann (bass),
Monteverdi Ch., English Baroque Soloists, Gardiner.
DG Dig. 431 806-2AH2.

DIE ZAUBERFLÖTE   K620

Ziesak (sop), Jo (sop), Heilmann (ten), Kraus (bar), Moll
(bass), Schmidt (bar), Zednik (ten), Leitner (sop),
Pieczonka (sop), Kuettenbaum, van Nes (mezs), Cencic, Rausch,
Leitner (trebs), Schmidt (ten), Franzen (bass), Bieber (ten), Porcher (bar),
Vienna Boys' Ch., Vienna State Opera Concert Ch., Vienna Philharmonic
Orch. Solti. Decca 433 210-2Dh2.

AAM *Academy of Ancient Music*
arr. *arranged/arrangement*
ASMF *Academy of St. Martin-in-the-Fields*
attrib. *attributed*
bar. *baritone*
bc. *basso continuo*
bn. *bassoon*
c. *circa*
ch. *chorus/choir/chorale*
Chan. *Chandos*
cl. *clarinet*
CO *Chamber Orchestra*
COE *Chamber Orchestra of Europe*
comp. *composed/composition*
contr. *contralto*
db. *double bass*
DG *Deutsche Grammophon*
Dig. *digital recording*
dir. *director*
ECO *English Chamber Orchestra*
ed. *editor/edited*
edn. *edition*
ens. *ensemble*
fl. *flute*
HM *Harmonia Mundi France*
hn. *horn*
hp. *harp*
hpd. *harpsichord*
Hung. *Hungaroton*

instr. *instrument/instrumental*
kbd. *keyboard*
LSO *London Symphony Orchestra*
Mer. *Meridian*
mez. *mezzo-soprano*
ob. *oboe*
OCO *Orpheus Chamber Orchestra*
orch. *orchestra/orchestral/orchestrated*
org. *organ/organist*
O-L *Oiseau-Lyre*
perc. *percussion*
pf. *pianoforte*
picc. *piccolo*
PO *Philharmonic Orchestra*
qnt. *quintet*
qt. *quartet*
sop. *soprano*
str. *string(s)*
tb. *trombone*
ten. *tenor*
tpt. *trumpet*
trans. *translated/translation*
transcr. *transcribed/transcription*
unacc. *unaccompanied*
va. *viola*
var. *various/variation*
vc. *cello*
vn. *violin*

- SELECTED FURTHER READING -

Emily Anderson ed., revised by Stanley Sadie & Fiona Smart,
The Letters of Mozart and his Family, 3rd edition (Macmillan   1989)

Volkmar Braunbehrens, *Mozart in Vienna* (Oxford University Press, 1991)

Otto Erich Deutsch, *Mozart: a documentary biography* (A & C Black, 1966)

Alfred Einstein, *Mozart: His Character, His Work* (Cassell, 1946)

Alex Hyatt King ed., *Mozart in Retrospect* (Thames & Hudson, 1970)

Wolfgang Hildesheimer, *Mozart* (J M Dent & Sons, 1988)

H C Robbins Landon ed., *The Mozart Compendium: a Guide to
Mozart's life and Music* (Thames & Hudson, 1991)

H C Robbins Landon, *Mozart: The Golden Years* (Thames & Hudson, 1989)

H C Robbins Landon, *1791: Mozart's Last Year* (Thames & Hudson, 1988)

Stanley Sadie, *The New Grove Mozart* (Papermac, 1982)

- ACKNOWLEDGEMENTS -

The publishers wish to thank the following copyright holders
for their permission to reproduce illustrations supplied:

Archiv Für Kunst und Geschichte, Berlin
The Bridgeman Art Library
The Mansell Collection Ltd

1. SINFONIA CONCERTANTE IN E♭ MAJOR, K364/320*d*, 1ST MOVEMENT   13'07"
   Arthur Grumiaux (violin), Arrigo Pellicia (viola)
   London Symphony Orchestra/Sir Colin Davis
   The sinfonia concertante for violin, viola and orchestra, probably dating from early 1779
   when the twenty-three-year-old composer was living in Salzburg, is one of Mozart's first
   undisputed masterpieces and one of his earliest works to find a regular place in the repertoire.

2. CLARINET CONCERTO IN A MAJOR, K622, 2ND MOVEMENT   7'17"
   Jack Brymer/London Symphony Orchestra
   Sir Colin Davis
   Written for his friend Anton Stadler, Mozart's concerto for clarinet and orchestra was
   completed only weeks before the composer's death and is one of the first large-scale works, as well
   as one of the best known, to exploit the potential of what was then a very new instrument.

3. PIANO CONCERTO NO. 23 IN A MAJOR, K488, 2ND MOVEMENT   7'01"
   Stephen Kovacevich/London Symphony Orchestra/Sir Colin Davis
   With the exception of opera, there was no other form Mozart so revolutionized as the piano
   concerto. Composed in Vienna in 1786 for his own performance, the slow movement of his
   twenty-third concerto, written in the unusual key of F♯ minor, shows the emotional intensity
   with which Mozart was able to infuse the dialogue between soloist and orchestra.

4. SERENADE FOR 13 INSTRUMENTS IN B♭ MAJOR, K361/370a, 3RD MOVEMENT   8'36"
Academy of St. Martin-in-the-Fields/Sir Neville Marriner
Also known as the 'gran partita', the serenade is a fine example of Mozart's wind writing,
which was transformed by his exposure to the Viennese Harmoniemusik *during his early*
years in the imperial capital, and is one of the crowning glories of the eighteenth century
serenade tradition.

5. STRING QUARTET NO. 17 IN B♭ MAJOR, 'HUNT', K458, 1ST MOVEMENT   8'47"
Italian Quartet
The fourth of the six string quartets Mozart dedicated to Joseph Haydn, the 'Hunt', so-called
because of the hunting motif on which the first movement is based, belies with its freshness and
vigour the 'long and painstaking labour' which went into their composition.

6. PIANO SONATA IN A MINOR, K310, 1ST MOVEMENT   8'52"
Claudio Arrau
One of the works that marks Mozart's coming of age as a composer, the A minor piano sonata
was written in Paris around the time of Mozart's mother's death in 1778.

7. REQUIEM, K626, DIES IRAE   1'44"
John Alldis Choir/BBC Symphony Orchestra/Sir Colin Davis
The result of an anonymous commission in 1791, the Requiem (mass for the dead) was
Mozart's last work and remained unfinished at his death. The 'Dies Irae' is an immensely
powerful evocation of the 'day of wrath', the final day on which, according to Catholic tradi-
tion, the living and the dead will be summoned to judgement.

8. *Don Giovanni,* K527, Or sai chi l'onore   3'10"
Martina Arroyo (soprano)
Orchestra of the Royal Opera House, Covent Garden/Sir Colin Davis
The second of the three operas on which Mozart worked with Lorenzo da Ponte, Don Giovanni, *first performed in Prague in 1787, is the story of a libertine who meets his nemesis when the spirit of one of his victims, the Commendatore, returns from the grave to drag him down to hell. In this aria the Commendatore's daughter, Donna Anna, whom the Don has seduced, calls on her fiancé to avenge her father's murder.*

9. *Die Zauberflöte,* K620, 'Bei Männern, welche Liebe fühlen '   3'02"
Margaret Price (soprano), Mikael Melbye (baritone)
Dresden Staatskapelle/Sir Colin Davis
Mozart's last opera Die Zauberflöte (The magic flute), *a tale of love, magic and initiation set within a masonic framework, proved immediately and enduringly popular after its first performance in 1791. In this perfectly balanced duet – an example of the concise beauty of Mozart's late style – the heroine Pamina and the birdcatcher Papageno sing of the transcendant love of man and wife.*

10. Symphony No. 41 in C major 'Jupiter', K551, 4th movement   6'47"
Royal Concertgebouw Orchestra/Josef Krips
The 'Jupiter' (a later nickname) is Mozart's last symphony and one of the three great symphonies written in a mere six weeks during the summer of 1788. The finale, which builds a towering contrapuntal edifice on the foundation of the four note theme stated at the beginning of the movement, is one of Mozart's greatest orchestral achievements.